LANA STENNER

FARM-FRESH
Charcuterie
SPREADS

TEN PEAKS PRESS®
EUGENE, OR

Author is represented by Jenni Burke of Illuminate Literacy Agency: www.illuminateliterary.com

Cover design by Molly von Borstel, Faceout Studio
Cover badge icon © PureSolution / Shutterstock
Interior design by Paul Nielsen, Faceout Studio

Farm-Fresh Charcuterie Spreads

Text and photography copyright © 2025 by Lana Stenner
Published by Ten Peaks Press, an imprint of Harvest House Publishers
Eugene, Oregon 97408

ISBN 978-0-7369-8917-6 (hardcover)
ISBN 978-0-7369-8918-3 (eBook)

Library of Congress Control Number: 2024939941

Printed in China

24 25 26 27 28 29 30 31 32 33 / RDS / 10 9 8 7 6 5 4 3 2 1

TO MY BELOVED PARENTS,

This book stands as a testament to the enduring legacy of your love and guidance that shaped every chapter of my life. I cherish the memories of our gatherings around a delicious spread of food, where joy and faith were shared. It has been my greatest privilege to be your daughter.

CONTENTS

FALL 83

WINTER 113

GRAZING INTO THE GOOD LIFE

Gathering with friends and family is one of our favorite things at the Grace-Filled Homestead. Over the last 20 years here on our property, we have curated a life around faith, family, and farm-fresh joy. Most of our local and online friends have gotten to know our silly little goats and feisty flock of birds, but the true joy comes as we are face-to-face, sharing our favorite foods. It's a good time in life to turn off the distracting screens, give an old friend a hug, and indulge in small bites of delicious cheese as we reconnect.

Nearly every meal and gathering around here starts with a beautiful board. Some are huge spreads, and others are fairly small. It could be placed at the kitchen island, outside on the patio, or even near the firepit. Just don't plan on picnicking in the goat pasture. They know how to crash a party and leave the tray clean in under 60 seconds.

Many of our charcuterie boards are filled with our favorite cheeses, cured meats, and crisp sliced veggies from the garden. It's more than just an appetizer before a meal; it's also an ice breaker to a nervous new boyfriend meeting the family for the first time or for distant relatives catching up over a tray of olives and nuts. Somehow, we have unexpectedly stumbled across the most beautiful balance of casual and relaxed entertaining, and yet at the same time it feels indulgent and elegant. Grazing on simple farm-fresh ingredients is a sign of the good life we all strive for. It doesn't get any better than sharing simple yet delicious foodie bites with your favorite people.

Life at the Grace-Filled Homestead is seasonal, and our beautiful boards will walk us through early spring veggies and emerging edible flowers. As the warm sun shines and the summer garden flourishes, our boards are filled with fresh fruits and delicious BBQ. When the crisp autumn harvest season arrives, our gatherings include cozy spreads filled with pumpkin spice fall flavors. Finally, the winter months are made for entertaining and holiday cheer. The festive charcuterie boards are filled with sugared cranberries, caprese salads in candy cane shapes, and all the *fromage* joy you can imagine.

Of course, some of our boards are playful and just plain silly. If it brings a smile to a three-year-old, we know it's a success. Please remember that when it comes to entertaining with boards, you are in a judgment-free zone. Allow the process to be joyful and simple. Get creative. I've included a few special articles to help you become a board master in no time and learn how to personalize the experience to suit your hosting style. If it brings you and your loved ones joy, add it in. Always remember: You are the board boss and can literally decide what makes the cut and what doesn't.

Use whatever type of board you want. Our favorites are wood, woven baskets, granite, slate, and glass. We find them in all shapes and sizes. Remember that the true star of the show is what you put on it. We've also found that edible flowers turn a normal spread into something extra special. So anytime you can grow or forage some blooms for your board, do so. Our favorites are pansies, violas, calendula, zinnias, roses, and lilacs, but the list goes on.

Farm-fresh grazing boards reflect the changing seasons and richness of the land. The simple ingredients combine to create a tapestry of flavors, textures, and aromas. They elevate your entertaining experience and, more importantly, allow for unforgettable moments with your family and friends. Let's get this party started.

A NOTE ABOUT SERVING SIZES

Charcuterie spreads are one of those beautiful things that do not require precision. I have included quantities that look nice together on a board for the start of your gathering, but depending on the crowd you are feeding, it may be good to have an extra stash on hand to refill the spread as needed. To the side of your main spread, you can also set up a nice bowl, platter, or tiered tray with additional cupcakes, crackers, or other elements of your spread that you think will be popular. Having extra quantities in the refrigerator to refill your spread is an especially good idea for items that will spoil or wilt if left out during a long gathering of snacking and celebrating, so that what you have on your board is always fresh. When planning quantities needed, consider your guests, don't overthink it, and have fun!

You are the board boss and can literally decide what makes the cut and what doesn't.

SPRING

As the last frost of winter melts, the homestead garden wakes with the promise of a bountiful season ahead. Spring is the season of renewal, marked by the joyous celebration of holidays such as St. Patrick's Day, Easter, and Mother's Day. These festive occasions provide an ideal opportunity to create vibrant and refreshing charcuterie boards as opening acts for your gatherings. Whether you're hosting a tea party or an engagement celebration, this chapter can help you set the tone for hospitality and joy.

The spring season on any homestead brings a large workload. Planting the gardens and spring-cleaning the barn and coop can be challenging. I share a breakfast board that brings together savory and sweet elements filled with hearty protein for chore-time energy. As the first cold-weather crops emerge through the soil, we are taking advantage of the timely produce and using it, for instance, as a creative cabbage bowl for holding light dips.

Occasionally the spring boards are so beautiful that your friends and family may hesitate to dig in, especially when it's a towering Cheese Wheel Engagement Cake or a tray of letter boxes filled with Mom's favorite treats. You can get the party started by assisting the guest of honor with their first taste of goodness. On the other hand, we've never had a problem getting the kiddos to start nibbling the Beautiful Bugs Garden Party board. It adds a whimsical touch to the festivities, incorporating edible flowers and playful insect-shaped delights. As adults, we should act more like the precious little ones who reach without hesitation for goodies on a beautiful board. Help your guests feel comfortable approaching your work of art with child-like wonder. A simple reminder such as, "Dig in, folks" is also a great icebreaker.

At the Grace-Filled Homestead, the charcuterie board becomes not just a culinary pleasure but also a reflection of the seasons that shape life on the farm and an opportunity to share hospitality with the ones you love. And like the spring season, spring gatherings showcase the colors, playfulness, and beauty that spark a sense of life and delight.

The charcuterie board becomes not
just a culinary pleasure but also a reflection
of the seasons that shape life on the farm
and an opportunity to share hospitality
with the ones you love.

WHAT IS CHARCUTERIE?

Charcuterie is a French word referring to cured meats such as prosciutto, pancetta, and salami sold in specialty preserved meat shops in France. Charcuterie traditionally referred to the art of preparing and preserving meats through methods like curing, smoking, and drying. Over time, especially here in America, the term has evolved to encompass broader culinary concepts beyond just meats. It now also refers to holiday spreads, sweet festive snacks, and gathering grazing boards. While the traditional charcuterie board showcased an array of cured meats, we love the American version at the Grace-Filled Homestead that embraces creativity, large farm gatherings, and garden-fresh ingredients.

We proudly break all the rules and add to our boards any fun bite-size treats we love, because when it comes down to what matters, the best gatherings are about bringing people together over wonderful food. And what serving style does that better than a charcuterie board?

The charm of a beautiful grazing board lies in its appeal to all the senses. Basic ingredients include an assortment of meats such as prosciutto, salami, and chorizo, complemented by an array of cheeses ranging from creamy brie, to sharp cheddar, and our favorite, goat cheese. Fruits like grapes, figs, and dried apricots add a burst of sweetness, while vegetables like cherry tomatoes and cucumber provide a refreshing crunch. Nuts, olives, pickles, and an assortment of crackers serve as perfect palate cleansers and textural contrasts. Dips, mustards, and other condiments act as flavor enhancers, offering a customizable experience for each guest. The beauty of these boards lies in their aesthetic appeal, some resembling a work of art as much as a culinary creation.

As we move through the calendar year, the seasons change and so do the contents of the charcuterie board. In the warmer months, lighter fare like edible flowers, fresh berries, and veggies take center stage, while heartier options like spiced nuts, thick-cut meats, and creamy cheeses dominate in the colder seasons. These boards are a timeless and cherished addition to gatherings, and they embody the essence of casual, communal dining and the pleasure of savoring an elegant array of flavors.

Grazing boards are amazingly casual, indulgent, and elegant at the same time!

EDIBLE-FLOWER BRIE
WITH CHERRY CHIPOTLE HUMMUS

Edible flowers are one of our favorite joys at the Grace-Filled Homestead. When you pair beautiful blooms with cheese, I believe the angels are singing in heaven. This simple treat is so easy to make and is a showstopper at any event. The Cherry Chipotle Hummus is filled with a depth of flavor you can't get enough of. The garden-fresh veggies go perfectly with the flavors of spring. This beautiful board will be empty within minutes!

BOARD DIRECTIONS

Rinse and dry all your fresh flowers and vegetables. To assemble the edible-flower brie, wet the outside rind of the brie with a dab of water. Choose your favorite edible flowers and press them down flat on the moistened outside edge of the brie. Wrap the cheese wedge with plastic wrap and place in the refrigerator for 2 hours. You can add 1 cup of the hummus to a bowl, then artfully arrange the fruit, veggies, nuts, crackers, and ham on your board with the hummus. Garnish with more edible flowers and basil leaves.

BOARD INGREDIENTS

6 oz. brie wedge

Fresh basil leaves and edible flowers

Cherry Chipotle Hummus *(recipe follows)*

6 radishes, sliced

3 celery ribs, sliced

1 cup sliced carrots

1 cup sugar snap peas

½ cup walnuts

6 strawberries

¾ cup broccoli florets

½ cup green olives

20 crackers

4 slices ham, cut in half and folded

CHERRY CHIPOTLE HUMMUS

DIRECTIONS

Combine all ingredients into a food processor and pulse until creamy and smooth. Add more olive oil as needed to reach your desired consistency. Add a few drops of hot sauce if you like it spicy. This sassy dip will take your veggies and crackers to the next level.

YIELD: 2 CUPS

INGREDIENTS

1 (15 oz.) can chickpeas, drained

¼ cup pickled beet juice

¼ cup tahini

¼ cup cherries, pitted and chopped

¼ tsp. chipotle powder or smoked paprika

2 T. olive oil

1 tsp. crushed garlic

½ tsp. salt

¼ tsp. black pepper

Hot sauce (optional)

SHAMROCK FRUIT RAINBOW

Your friends and family will be the lucky ones when they get to snack on the produce and chocolate on this whimsical board. As we celebrate the Irish folklore of leprechauns and pots of gold at the end of the rainbow, we'll be crafting our very own edible treasure. Whether you're hosting a festive gathering or simply looking to brighten your day, this St. Patrick's Day–themed board promises to be a delightful centerpiece that's as fun to make as it is to devour.

BOARD INGREDIENTS

2 cups strawberries, tops removed

1 cup raspberries

2 cups cantaloupe chunks

2 cups pineapple chunks

2 cups green grapes

1 cup blueberries

1 cup blackberries

2 bananas, sliced in rounds

5 gold foil–wrapped chocolate coins or Rolo candies

3 green bell peppers

BOARD DIRECTIONS

Prepare your produce by rinsing, drying, peeling, and slicing as needed. Begin making the outer arch shape of the rainbow by arranging the red strawberries and raspberries. Continue the next three layers of the half circle by arranging the cantaloupe, pineapple, and grapes. Then finish off the interior arch shape with the blueberries and blackberries. Add the banana slices to one end of the rainbow in the shape of a cloud, and add the chocolate coins or Rolos to the other end for a pot of gold. Slice the bottom inch off of the three peppers and remove any attached membranes or seeds. For the shamrock stems, cut three 1-inch-long slivers from the top of the pepper. Place the pepper bottoms and stems under the rainbow for a fun and spicy four-leaf clover. Let the celebration begin!

CABBAGE, HUMMUS, AND BLUE CHEESE BOARD

This farm-fresh cabbage and blue cheese board is filled with early spring garden goodness. Cabbage is one of our first harvests of the season, and it's so fun to fill it with creamy hummus dip. The olives, cheeses, and veggies make a healthy treat you can feel good about.

BOARD DIRECTIONS

Rinse and dry your produce and slice into bite-size pieces as desired. Cut the cabbage in half, and use a spoon to remove some of the inside to make a bowl from one of the halves. Fill the cabbage cavity with hummus, a scattering of chickpeas, and a drizzle of olive oil. Next, add the two cheeses at opposite sides of the board, as well as the two varieties of olives. Fill in the rest of the space with the grapes, veggies, crackers, and honeycomb. Garnish with pansies or your favorite edible blooms.

BOARD INGREDIENTS

1 small red cabbage

1 cup prepared hummus

2 T. chickpeas

1 T. olive oil

4 oz. wedge blue cheese

5 mini squares cheddar

½ cup green olives

½ cup kalamata olives

2 clusters green grapes

2 radishes

¼ cup pickled red onions

¼ cup cherry tomatoes

¼ cup broccoli florets

¼ cup carrots

½ cup sugar snap peas

1 cup crackers or bruschetta rounds

1 small square honeycomb

Pansies or other edible flowers, for garnish

RESURRECTION DAY CHARCUTERIE

We love to gather for a special Resurrection Sunday brunch after church. It's so fun to see the little ones dressed up and full of sugar energy. Faith, family, and the farm have always been our focus at the Grace-Filled Homestead, and this festive board helps us celebrate our Savior, spring blooms, and baby birds. It's filled with delicious veggies, meats, candies, and our adorable deviled eggs in the shape of baby chicks. The final touch is our Bird's Nest Cookies that are beyond delicious. Your Sunday guests will appreciate this special spread. This faith-inspired board would also be a wonderful addition to other celebrations such as a baptism or graduation baccalaureate.

BOARD INGREDIENTS

1 cucumber

1 kiwi

3 slices cheddar cheese

3 slices pepper jack cheese

½ cup strawberries

½ cup raspberries

½ cup pineapple chunks

½ cup baby carrots

1 cup chocolate egg candies

Bird's Nest Cookies
(recipe follows)

8 slices smoked turkey

15 crackers

10 tortilla pinwheels (prepared)

4 iced cookies

Hatching Chicks Deviled Eggs
(recipe follows)

BOARD DIRECTIONS

Rinse and dry your produce as needed. Slice the cucumber into rounds, and peel and slice the kiwi into rounds. Use mini flower-shaped cookie cutters to cut the cucumber slices and cheddar cheese slices into bloom shapes. I use a small round cutter to cut circles from the pepper jack cheese and place the circles on top of the cheddar daisies for a simple, elevated look.

Start your board by arranging some items to form the exterior shape of the cross. We used the cucumbers and cheese, then added fruit, carrots, chocolate eggs, and six of the Bird's Nest Cookies. Don't overthink it. Have fun placing your goodies wherever you want. Fill in the shape with the turkey, crackers, pinwheels, cookies, and six of the deviled eggs. Additional goodies can be set aside to restock the display as needed. What a special treat for your Sunday brunch!

BIRD'S NEST COOKIES

INGREDIENTS

1 cup creamy peanut butter
1½ cups butterscotch chips
4 cups chow mein noodles
36 mini chocolate Easter eggs

DIRECTIONS

In a medium saucepan over low heat, combine peanut butter and butterscotch chips. Stir until melted and smooth. In a large mixing bowl, combine chow mein noodles and melted peanut butter mixture. Stir until noodles are coated. Divide the cookie mixture evenly into a 12-slot greased muffin tin. Press down in the middle of each cookie to make an indentation for the candy eggs. Place the muffin tin in the fridge to chill for at least 30 minutes, until the cookies are hard. Gently remove each cookie from the pan with a butter knife and place three candy eggs on top (I find that Cadbury eggs, M&M eggs, or Hershey eggs all work well).

YIELD: 12 COOKIES

HATCHING CHICKS DEVILED EGGS

DIRECTIONS

Cut each hard-boiled egg to shape the chicks: One at a time, place an egg on its side on a cutting board. Make one cut, barely shaving off the bottom, so the egg will sit upright and flat. Make the second cut on each egg closer to the pointed top, taking off the top like a lid. Save the lids.

With a small spoon, carefully remove the yolks and place them in a bowl. Use a fork to finely smash the yolks. Blend the egg yolks with the Dijon mustard and white vinegar to a thick, smooth consistency. I use my stand mixer for this. Add the mayonnaise, salt, and pepper, beating until smooth. Transfer the mixture into a piping bag. Fill each egg white cup generously above the cavity.

Build a small face for each baby chick: For the eyes, cut the olives into small pieces and place them with kitchen tweezers. For the beaks, cut twelve small triangles from a baby carrot and place on each chick's face. Place the egg white tops above the face like a hat. Arrange the deviled eggs on the board with the flat side down. Enjoy!

YIELD: 12 HATCHING CHICKS

INGREDIENTS

12 hard-boiled eggs, cooled and peeled

2 tsp. Dijon mustard

2 T. white vinegar

½ cup mayonnaise

¼ tsp. salt

¼ tsp. pepper

2 black olives

1 small carrot

FARM-FRESH FROMAGE FONDUE

We love our cheeses around here, and it's hard to beat a Swiss and Gruyère fondue. Although this board is wonderful as an appetizer, it is substantial and special enough to be the main event of your evening when you add meat and bread to your favorite veggie tray. This offering brings your friends and family close as you all gather around the fondue pot to dip and share the goodies. If you don't have a traditional fondue pot, you can easily melt your fondue on the stove and add the pot directly to your board.

BOARD DIRECTIONS

Rinse and dry your veggies and cut into bite-size pieces as desired. Bring together the breads, meat, veggies, and your guests. Artfully arrange all ingredients around the star of the show: the fondue. Is there anything better than sharing your favorite Fromage Fondue with friends and family? Enjoy!

FROMAGE FONDUE

DIRECTIONS

Combine the Gruyère and Swiss cheeses with the wine, cornstarch, and lemon juice in your fondue pot or a medium saucepan. Cook over medium heat, stirring occasionally, until the cheeses begin to melt, about 5 minutes. Reduce heat to low. Add the garlic, mustard, a generous pinch each of pepper and nutmeg, and cook, stirring gently, until creamy and smooth, about 3 minutes. Don't overcook the fondue or the consistency will change. Serve immediately.

YIELD: 8 SERVINGS

BOARD INGREDIENTS

10 mini sweet peppers

1 cup broccoli florets

1 cup cauliflower florets

2 cups Pumpernickel bread cubes

2 cups French bread cubes

2 cups ham cubes

4 cups Fromage Fondue
  (recipe follows)

INGREDIENTS

1 lb. Gruyère cheese, grated

½ lb. Swiss cheese, grated

1 cup white wine (the alcohol will cook out)

1 T. plus 1 tsp. cornstarch

1 tsp. lemon juice

1 T. crushed garlic

2 tsp. Dijon mustard

Black pepper

Freshly grated nutmeg

TEA PARTY TIME

The simple tradition of teatime can make an ordinary day extra special. The rustic charm of the countryside meets the elegance of a classic tea party in this tasty lineup for lunch, brunch, or afternoon break. Whether you are in a fragrant garden listening to the sweet melodies of birds or you are escaping the office chatter and traffic noises, pausing for tea will bring you joy.

The centerpiece for this board is the Lemon Lilac Scones. They have a blend of zesty citrus and earthy floral flavors. Complementing the scones are traditional Cucumber Tea Sandwiches. The thinly sliced cucumbers paired with a luscious herbed spread creates a balance of textures and tastes to offset all the sweet tea treats. Get ready to invite your besties to wear their fancy hats, or welcome your favorite three-year-old and her teddy bear.

BOARD INGREDIENTS

6 tea bags of choice

6 cups hot water

12 Cucumber Tea Sandwiches
(recipe follows)

12 Lemon Lilac Scones
(recipe follows)

12 macarons

6 tea biscuit cookies

12 rolled crème filled wafer cookies
(we use Pepperidge Farms
Pirouettes)

Lilac blooms, for garnish

BOARD DIRECTIONS

Steep each tea bag in a cup of hot water for 15 minutes. Serve in mismatched china and vintage teacups to make your party memorable. Layer your board with the cucumber sandwiches and scones first, then add in all the cookies. Garnish with edible lilac blooms.

CUCUMBER TEA SANDWICHES

INGREDIENTS

4 oz. cream cheese, softened

1 T. mayonnaise

1 tsp. fresh dill, chopped

1 tsp. fresh chives, chopped

¼ tsp. garlic powder

Salt and pepper

1 cucumber, rinsed, peeled, and thinly sliced

6 slices bread, crusts removed

DIRECTIONS

Mix cream cheese and mayonnaise in a small bowl until smooth. Stir in herbs and garlic powder, and add salt and pepper to taste. Spread cream cheese mixture and a layer of cucumbers on three bread slices, topping each sandwich with the other three slices of bread. Cut each sandwich into four triangles.

YIELD: 12 TEA SANDWICHES

LEMON LILAC SCONES

INGREDIENTS

1 stick (8 T.) butter

¾ cup milk

¼ cup fresh lemon juice

½ tsp. vanilla

¼ cup sugar

2 T. lemon zest

2½ cups flour

1 T. baking powder

½ tsp. baking soda

½ tsp. salt

2½ tsp. organic lilac flower buds, plus more for garnish

ICING INGREDIENTS

1 cup powdered sugar

1 T. milk

1 tsp. lemon zest

DIRECTIONS

Cut the butter into small cubes and place in the freezer. Preheat the oven to 375°F. Line a baking sheet with parchment paper.

Combine the milk, lemon juice, and vanilla. In a separate bowl, whisk together the sugar and lemon zest, then add in the flour, baking powder, baking soda, salt, and lilacs. Using a pastry blender, cut the butter into the flour mixture until pea-size clumps form. Stir together the milk and flour mixtures until just combined.

Transfer the dough to a floured surface and form it into a ball, being careful not to overwork the dough. Press the dough into an 8 × 5-inch rectangle. Cut the rectangle down the middle, lengthwise, to have two long rectangles. Then make two cuts, to create six squares. Cut each square in half diagonally to form two triangles. This will result in twelve small triangle scones.

Transfer the scones to the baking sheet with a spatula, spacing them three inches apart. Bake for 20 minutes until the bottoms and tops are slightly golden brown. Remove and let them cool. Stir together the icing ingredients until combined. Drizzle icing on completely cooled scones and garnish with organic lilac blooms.

YIELD: 12 SMALL SCONES

MOTHER'S DAY LOVE LETTERS

We treasure our mommas at the Grace-Filled Homestead. Whether we call you Nannie, Meema, or just plain Mom, you deserve an extra special treat on Mother's Day. Occasionally you can find true charcuterie letters or numbers already cut out at your local craft stores, but no worries if you can't. Grab your crafting knife, cut around the top of the cardboard letter edges, and remove any support pieces inside to give you plenty of space to pamper the special lady in your life.

BOARD DIRECTIONS

Start by lining the inside of each letter with colored tissue or parchment paper. This step is optional; however, it does make the display prettier and keeps the letters cleaner. I like to start by placing the olives in small serving bowls and setting these inside the letters. I then fill in the spaces in the letters with the meats, cheeses, and nuts, followed by the rest of the treats. To make it extra special, add a few of Mom's favorite seasonal blooms as a garnish. What a wonderful way to honor the amazing women in your life.

The combination of letters or numbers is endless. Of course, you can also use a number board to celebrate a special birthday. When our favorite three-year-old had a birthday this year, we ordered fancy cupcakes for her friends and filled in the rest of the areas with her favorite treats. It was a hit! One of my best friends used charcuterie numbers at her daughter's graduation party.

BOARD INGREDIENTS

Colored tissue paper or parchment paper (optional)

1 cup green olives

1 cup kalamata olives

24 pepperoni slices

24 salami slices

1 cup Colby-Jack cheese cubes

1 cup cheddar cheese cubes

1 cup cashews

12 lemon sandwich cookies

12 mini cookies

6 mini strawberry Bundt cakes (we use Hostess Baby Bundts)

1 cup pretzels

3 mini blueberry muffins

1 cup popcorn

Edible blooms (optional)

BEAUTIFUL BUGS GARDEN PARTY

This critter board will put a smile on the face of anyone who sees it.

BOARD DIRECTIONS

Assemble each type of bug as directed below and set aside.

To make the snails, spread peanut butter in the inside cavity of the celery. Cut celery into two pieces. For each celery piece, place a cucumber slice upright in the peanut butter, and use chive pieces for the antennae. Stand the Cheerios up for the eyes.

The dragonfly body is made from snap peas; cut the wings out of orange peppers and again place Cheerios for the eyes.

The ladybugs are always a hit around here. Start by simply placing half of a cherry tomato on a slice of mozzarella. Cut the end off a black olive for the head, then use a toothpick to add dots of balsamic glaze to the tomatoes for the ladybug spots.

To make the bees, alternate slices of the green and black olives and add almond sliver wings.

Prepare the Sweet and Savory Dip but don't combine the dip with the crushed sandwich cookies yet: Spread the cream cheese mixture evenly across the bottom fourth of your board.

In the top half of the board, place ranch dressing in a small bowl, and place yellow pepper slices around it to form a sunflower. Add your bugs onto the board. Garnish with chives, mint, basil, and edible flowers. Add a bowl of pretzel sticks for dipping.

BOARD INGREDIENTS

1 T. peanut butter

1 (6 inch) celery rib

2 cucumber slices

Chive stems of varying lengths

12 Cheerios

4 sugar snap peas

1 orange bell pepper

4 cherry tomatoes

3 slices fresh mozzarella

4 large black olives

1 tsp. balsamic glaze

2 large green olives

4 almond slivers

Sweet and Savory Dip
  (recipe follows)

¼ cup ranch dressing

1 yellow bell pepper, sliced
  evenly into strips

Mint

Fresh basil leaves

5 edible flowers such as pansies

Pretzel sticks for dipping (optional)

SWEET AND SAVORY DIP

DIRECTIONS

Combine softened cream cheese, garlic, and dill.

Crush the sandwich cookies (such as Oreos). Add a thin layer of cookie crumbles over the cream cheese mixture for a touch of sweetness and the appearance of dirt for a bug- or garden-themed spread.

YIELD: ½ CUP

INGREDIENTS

4 oz. cream cheese, softened

½ tsp. crushed garlic

½ tsp. dill

4 to 6 chocolate sandwich
  cookies, crushed

CHICKEN AND WAFFLES BREAKFAST

Breakfast in bed can be so easy, especially if it is served on a board. Chicken and waffles is a favorite around here. The crisp and tender chicken with the sweetness of pastry and syrup creates a delicious treat to start your weekend right. Or once you taste this, it may become a mid-week indulgence too.

BOARD INGREDIENTS

2 chicken tenders (breaded, precooked, about 2 oz. each)

2 Belgian waffles (prepared or frozen)

2 soft-boiled eggs

4 cups coffee (French press directions below)

2 pipettes, for serving

4 T. maple syrup

1 cup strawberries, rinsed and dried

2 cups fresh orange juice

BOARD DIRECTIONS

The preparation of this board is made simpler by using premade chicken tenders and Belgian waffles. Heat the chicken and waffles according to package directions, then start in on the eggs.

We like our eggs soft-boiled and served in egg cups. To prepare soft-boiled eggs, bring a small saucepan of water to a boil (enough water to cover the eggs), then add the eggs and cook for 6 minutes. Remove the eggs from the hot water with a slotted spoon and place them in your egg cups.

While you are boiling the eggs, it's time to start the coffee. To make in a French press, first warm a 4-cup French press under hot water. Coarsely grind 4 tablespoons of coffee beans and place the grounds in the bottom of the press. Add 4 cups of boiling water, stir, and put the lid on without pressing down. After 4 minutes, press down, and your coffee is ready to pour.

To serve, place a warm chicken tender on top of each waffle and place on the board. Fill empty pipettes by squeezing the air out and adding the tip into the syrup, backfilling the pipette with the sweet natural goodness. Place the syrup pipette on top of the waffle. Add the eggs in egg cups to your tray, and fill in the board with strawberries, glasses of orange juice, and cups of coffee. You are going to have a great day!

CHEESE WHEEL
ENGAGEMENT CAKE

It was love at first sight for me! This indulgent board will make any celebration memorable. We brought this masterpiece to my niece's engagement party, but it also would fit right in at a wedding, shower, or birthday party. The concept is so simple and the visual is extravagant. We have two nationally known artisan cheese shops in our state and decided to take a short road trip to pick out our favorite fromage flavors. Although we decided on three layers, you could go down to only two or as high as four.

BOARD DIRECTIONS

The bottom layer of the cheese cake is the large wheel of Gouda wrapped in wax. Once the wax is removed, place the Gouda on a sturdy cake stand. The middle layer is the mini Swiss wheel centered on top of the Gouda. Add the French blue cheese wheel as the top layer.

Once the cheese wheels are in place, add a satin ribbon around the bottom layer and secure the ribbon with a straight pin. Add three roses to the top layer, and add rose leaves between the layers as a garnish. This cake is so beautiful that your guests may not want to be the first to cut into this masterpiece. Of course, cheese is for eating, so make that first cut with a sturdy knife, and serve with grapes and crackers.

BOARD INGREDIENTS

14-lb. wheel Gouda cheese

5-lb. wheel mini Swiss cheese

2.25-lb. wheel French blue cheese

1 yard satin ribbon

Roses and leaves, for garnish

Grapes and assorted crackers, for serving

SUMMER

Welcome to the radiant embrace of summer on the homestead! As the sun extends its warm rays across the goat pasture, our gardens burst forth with an abundance of vibrant colors and fragrant blossoms. Summer is a season of growth, joy, and the simple pleasures of life, and what better way to celebrate this lively season than with a charming homestead garden-fresh charcuterie board?

As the school doors close and laughter fills the air, children embark on their cherished summer vacation, eager to explore the wonders of the great outdoors. It's a time when the farm becomes a playground, and our kitchen transforms into a haven of culinary adventures. Amid the festivities, there's an undeniable allure to crafting a simple yet delightful charcuterie board, an activity that effortlessly aligns with the carefree spirit of summer.

Some of our most memorable boards appear in this chapter, including the vertical donut wall. It can be a fun addition to any brunch or shower, and hello...it's filled with donuts! Is there anything better? A fun-filled "snackle box" makes a wonderful gift for Father's Day and can also be used as a portable charcuterie loaded with your favorite snacks to take to the beach or park.

A traditional lobster boil is always a fun summer activity, and cheers to a one-pot meal served on a board. And finally, summer and ice cream go hand in hand. Our sundae board can cool off the steamiest summer days.

Summer calls for celebrations, and what's more festive than enjoying a BBQ, relaxing at a poolside soirée, or commemorating cherished occasions like Father's Day and the Fourth of July? This chapter is a symphony of summer sensations, a collection of boards that mirror the season's effervescent energy.

Summer on the homestead is not just a season; it's a celebration of life, love, and the bountiful harvests that grace our tables. Join us in embracing the warmth of the sun, the laughter of loved ones, and the irresistible charm of a Grace-Filled Homestead garden-fresh charcuterie board. Let the summer feasts begin!

Summer on the homestead is not just a season; it's a celebration of life, love, and the bountiful harvests that grace our tables.

BEAUTIFUL BLOOMS AND EDIBLE FLOWERS

Throughout history, edible flowers have been used in baking, and I can see why. Whether you are a foodie, homesteader, or backyard gardener, we know these blooms take our food experience to the next level. We've been using edible flowers in the Grace-Filled Homestead kitchen for years, and they make a perfect addition to a charcuterie board or gathering spread. The beautiful blooms enhance the flavors and aesthetic of your spreads while making them feel extra special.

Some flowers are edible, and others are not. So, it's important to make sure that you have identified them properly. It's also important to eat blooms that have not been sprayed with pesticides or even been foraged from unfamiliar environments. I prefer to grow my own edible flowers or use local friends and farms so I know about their growing process. Edible flowers will fill your gathering space with wonderful floral aromas. Like your fruits, veggies, and herbs, these blooms are packed with nutrients and are used for medicinal purposes as well. Many of them have vitamins A, C, D, E, and K, as well as B vitamins like folate, thiamine, and riboflavin. They may also contain healthy elements like potassium, magnesium, copper, flavonoids, beta-carotene, lutein, lycopene, linoleic acid, iron, calcium, as well as protein, antioxidants, and fiber.

Homeopathic doctors, homesteaders, and many grandmas love to use these edible flowers in their tinctures and concoctions for whatever ails the ones they care for. Whether your blooms are part of a scone recipe or added as a garnish, edible flowers are a perfect addition to your beautiful boards.

Pansies are my all-time favorite. The plants love the cooler temps and are one of the first blooms in early spring, lasting late into early winter. Pansies have a sweet grassy flavor. Use edible pansies in cakes, cocktails, desserts, soups, salads, or as a garnish. My favorite way to present pansies is pressed on top of a sugar cookie.

Zinnias are known for their ability to brighten any room they adorn with their bold colors and large, soft petals. Zinnias have a long flowering season beginning in early summer and ending around the first frost of fall, which means you can have fresh flowers for months on end. As zinnias have a rather bitter flavor, I recommend their bright petals be used as a colorful garnish rather than a main ingredient. However, their blooms can be used to season a salad, freshen a tea, flavor a soup or stew, or embellish desserts or bread.

Lilacs are more than sweet, fragrant additions to your garden; they are also perfectly safe to eat. In the cool months of spring, I like to start off my day by taking a walk in my garden to enjoy the lovely smell of lilacs and forage their petals for an afternoon dessert. Their taste is sweetly floral with a hint of citrus. Lilacs are often used to infuse sugar or syrup, which can be added into countless springtime recipes. However, one of my favorite ways to use these beautiful blooms is to add them directly into different dessert mixes and to use them as a lovely garnish on cakes, donuts, and scones.

Bee balm is a favorite plant among hummingbirds, bees, and butterflies, making it a perfect addition to any garden even without its edible properties. The flavor is minty with a slight hint of orange. Both the leaves and flowers of bee balm can be eaten raw or cooked, used as an oregano substitute, or made into a tea that can help aid digestion. The blue, purple, and pink blooms make a beautiful garnish on your boards in spring.

Chamomile is widely known for its powerful medicinal uses, soothing properties, and simple growing demands. These popular flowers feature delicate white petals, bright yellow centers, and tender leaves, which are all edible and easy to forage. Chamomile's flavor is sweet and similar to apples. Chamomile flowers are commonly used to make sweet, soothing tea, but can also be used as a topping on desserts or salads.

Peonies are often overlooked when it comes to edible flowers, but they certainly deserve to make the list. They are actually considered an herb, taste just like they smell, and their roots have been used in traditional Chinese medicine for centuries. Their flavor is sweet, similar to peaches or strawberries. Peony flowers are used most often to make jellies, syrups, and cocktails. Not only do they add a delicious, sweet flavor to these recipes but also add a natural pink hue to them as well. Peonies are always in bloom on Mother's Day here at the Grace-Filled Homestead, so they are an obvious addition to any board honoring your precious momma.

More than anything, I must have flowers, always, and always.

Claude Monet

DONUT WALL AND SPRINKLE SHOOTERS

If you are looking to level up your entertaining, add a donut wall. This new trend has become popular for good reason. It's a space saver, as well as a wonderful addition to a self-serving brunch spread. We used a vertical board for a recent baby shower, and it was the hit of the party. Your guests can easily reach for the treat they want.

This serving option is simple, versatile, and fun, so let's get started building your donut wall. You can easily do this yourself!

DONUT WALL

BOARD DIRECTIONS

To make your own donut wall, first decide on the size you want. The measurements specified here are for a 24-inch square. We had a chunky gold frame in the storage room and decided to touch up the finish with rose gold paint. You can also simply use a piece of plywood without a frame. We painted the front of the plywood and secured it in the frame using the frame's attached hardware.

We have nine dowels centered 6 inches apart. Using a tape measure, mark the dowel locations with a pencil. Drill the holes with a ½-inch bit all the way through to the back of the plywood. Lay the donut wall flat on its back. Add a minimal amount of wood glue to the end of one dowel, and place it in the drilled hole, wiping any excess glue off with a wet towel. Continue until all the dowels are inserted in the holes on your board. Let the glue dry and set overnight. Wipe the donut wall and dowels down to sanitize it before adding donuts

Once your donut wall is assembled, dried, and cleaned, place nine bakery or homemade donuts on the wall. Have an additional tray of donuts nearby to restock the wall as your delicious treats disappear. Set up your Chocolate Milk Sprinkle Shooters and any additional cookies and treats you'd like to have for your gathering. Enjoy!

BOARD SUPPLIES

24-inch square frame

2 ft. × 2 ft. plywood, ½-inch thick, painted

9 dowels (½ inch × 6 inch), painted

Tape measure

Electric drill with ½-inch drill bit

Wood glue

BOARD INGREDIENTS

Donuts (from your favorite shop)

Chocolate-dipped cookies (homemade or purchased)

Pudding, fruit, and other treats as desired

Strawberry Fields Donuts *(recipe follows)*

Chocolate Milk Sprinkle Shooters *(recipe follows)*

STRAWBERRY FIELDS DONUTS

INGREDIENTS

2 cups flour

⅔ cup sugar

2 tsp. baking powder

½ tsp. cinnamon

¼ tsp. salt

⅔ cup milk

2 eggs

2 T. butter, softened

20 medium strawberries

1 T. seedless strawberry jam

GLAZE INGREDIENTS

3 cups powdered sugar

3 T. strawberry jam

½ cup cold milk

DIRECTIONS

Preheat oven to 425°F. Grease two donut pans with cooking spray. Each pan should have six cavities. To make donuts, combine dry ingredients in a large bowl and whisk together. Create a well in the center of the dry ingredients and add the milk, eggs, and butter. Stir until well combined.

Rinse your strawberries and remove any stems or leaves. Use a food processor to puree the strawberries and jam, then stir the strawberry mixture into the batter. The batter should be wet but not runny. Put the dough into a pastry bag, and pipe batter into each well, filling just over half full. Bake for 7 to 9 minutes or until donuts spring back when touched. Let cool 5 minutes before carefully removing the donuts from the pan and placing them on a cooling rack to cool completely. To make the glaze, whisk all ingredients together until smooth and then drizzle evenly on top of the donuts.

YIELD: 12 DONUTS

CHOCOLATE MILK SPRINKLE SHOOTERS

INGREDIENTS

8 oz. chocolate melting wafers (we use strawberry wafers)

12 tall 2-oz. shooter glasses

¼ cup rainbow sprinkles

3 cups chocolate milk

6 decorative paper straws, cut in half

DIRECTIONS

Melt the chocolate wafers on the stovetop on low, preferably using a double boiler, stirring continuously for approximately 3 minutes or until most of the pieces are melted; remove from heat and stir until smooth. Dip the rim of each glass into the chocolate. Before letting it cool, sprinkle the rainbow sprinkles onto the warm chocolate. Sit shooter glasses upright to cool. To serve, add chocolate milk and a decorative paper straw.

YIELD: 12 SHOOTERS

FATHER'S DAY SNACKLE BOX

For Father's Day this year, we wanted to treat Grandpa right with a fun but memorable treat. He has always loved fishing, and he has tackle boxes filled to the brim with all his hooks, bait, fishing line, spools, and bobbers. A snackle box is a wonderful container filled with all your char-cuterie snacks to go. The multiple compartments are the perfect size to fit your favorite treats. A snackle box is also a great idea for a day at the beach, kids' sporting events, or picnics in the park. You can also use the bottom compartment as a mini drink cooler.

BOARD DIRECTIONS

To assemble the snackle box, first add your drinks to the bottom container and cover with ice. On the first tray, add pepperoni slices, folded in half and stacked in a row. Add the cheese, meat, crackers, and pretzels. The celery, pickles, olives, pecans, and grapes offer a few healthy options; add these to the next level. Finally, add in a few of your chocolate pieces for dessert. Although it's not an insulated cooler, the ice in the bottom keeps the items fresh for a couple of hours. Feel free to customize your snacks for an extra special day outside.

BOARD INGREDIENTS

1 new tackle box with multiple compartments

2 cans root beer (appropriately, we like Dad's root beer)

1 cup ice

12 pepperoni slices

8 slices cheddar

4 slices pepper jack

6 meat sticks

1½ cups cheese crackers

1 cup pretzels

2 celery ribs, washed, dried, and sliced

½ cup baby pickles

½ cup olives

½ cup pecans

2 clusters grapes, rinsed and dried

½ cup chocolate-covered peanuts

10 chocolate truffles

STARS AND STRIPES CHARCUTERIE

A patriotic charcuterie board is a simple and festive addition to your holiday celebrations. Whether you are having a Labor Day or Memorial Day picnic, a Fourth of July swim party, or an election watch party, you can't go wrong with a delicious tray of cheeses, meats, olives, nuts, and fruits. This year we decided to change it up by adding a yummy Blueberry Goat Cheese Dip.

BOARD INGREDIENTS

Blueberry Goat Cheese Dip
(recipe follows)

4 provolone slices

1 cup pistachios in the shell

½ cup olives

24 crackers

1 cup blueberries, rinsed and dried

2 cups strawberries, rinsed and dried

6 slices turkey, rolled

8 slices salami, quartered

BOARD DIRECTIONS

I am a self-proclaimed cheese addict and can't imagine a charcuterie board without at least two different cheese options. The star of this show is a bowl of Blueberry Goat Cheese Dip in the middle of your board. Next, create patriotic cheese stars. We used a small cookie cutter to form stars from slices of the provolone cheese.

Bring in more star shapes by using a specialty star-shaped bowl for your dip. Layer the nuts, olives, and crackers around the dip, then place the fruit and meat. Finally, add your patriotic provolone stars across the board. This beautiful and tasty board will be a memorable treat to celebrate our country.

BLUEBERRY GOAT CHEESE DIP

INGREDIENTS

4 oz. goat cheese

½ cup blueberries, rinsed and dried

1 T. powdered sugar

DIRECTIONS

Slightly warm and soften goat cheese in a bowl so it has a creamy texture. Mix in the blueberries, and add powdered sugar for sweetness. Stir carefully and spoon into a small serving dish, or form into a roll and chill before adding it to your board.

YIELD: 1 CUP

FIESTA TACO BAR WITH PEACH SALSA

This is a happy board that is on our regular rotation for meals at the Grace-Filled Homestead. This spread is our main course and is always a hit. The showstopper is our Sweet and Spicy Peach Salsa made from fresh peaches and classic Mexican ingredients. Of course, you have to offer a creamy queso dip for a true fiesta taco bar. This Queso Blanco Dip is scrumptious, and you will want to drizzle this goodness on everything. I do love this container board that allows us to keep the meat and the cheese dip warm while all the other ingredients stay at room temperature.

BOARD DIRECTIONS

First, add the pantry ingredients to the board, such as the chips, shells, and tortillas. Next, add your fresh fruit, veggies, cilantro, and sour cream. Fill this in with containers of guacamole, salsa, and shredded cheese. Finally, add the warm, creamy queso and seasoned meat. Enjoy!

BOARD INGREDIENTS

2 cups tortilla chips
(plus more to refill)

6 to 12 crunchy taco shells

12 mini flour tortillas for soft tacos

1 lime, sliced

1 cup romaine lettuce, chopped

1 cup cherry tomatoes

½ cup red onion, chopped

½ cup pickled jalapeños

¼ cup black olives, sliced

Cilantro bunch

½ cup sour cream

1 cup guacamole

2 cups Sweet and Spicy Peach Salsa *(recipe follows)*

2 cups shredded Colby and pepper jack mix

2 cups Queso Blanco Dip *(recipe follows)*

Seasoned Meat *(recipe follows)*

SEASONED MEAT

DIRECTIONS

Brown ground beef in a skillet on medium heat and drain off the grease. Add taco seasoning and Worcestershire sauce and let brown an additional 2 minutes.

INGREDIENTS

1 lb. ground beef

2 T. taco seasoning mix

2 T. Worcestershire sauce

YIELD: 8 SERVINGS

SWEET AND SPICY PEACH SALSA

INGREDIENTS

2 large fresh peaches, diced

2 large tomatoes, diced

¼ cup cilantro, chopped

1 lime, zested and juiced

1 fresh jalapeño, seeded and diced

¼ tsp. smoked paprika

2 cloves garlic, minced

½ tsp. salt

¼ tsp. pepper

DIRECTIONS

Add peaches, tomatoes, cilantro, lime juice and zest, jalapeños, paprika, garlic, salt, and pepper to a mixing bowl. Gently combine and place in the refrigerator for 1 hour before serving.

YIELD: 8 SERVINGS

QUESO BLANCO DIP

DIRECTIONS

Place the cheese, milk, and butter in a saucepan over low heat, stirring frequently until melted. Stir in the green chilis, cumin, garlic salt, cayenne pepper, and smoked paprika. Add additional milk, if desired, for a thinner consistency.

YIELD: 8 SERVINGS

INGREDIENTS

1 lb. white American cheese

½ cup milk

2 T. butter

2 (4 oz.) cans green chilis

½ tsp. cumin

½ tsp. garlic salt

¼ tsp. cayenne pepper

½ tsp. smoked paprika

PINEAPPLE POOL PARTY

It's time to beat the summer heat and dive into a world of sweet indulgence with our Pineapple Pool Party board. This centerpiece will make your pool party unforgettable. The sweet creamy dip that resembles a refreshing pool even has a couple of Teddy Graham friends floating in sweet peach ring candies. Your guests can dip their fruit in the sweet blue dip and then into the graham cracker sand. Don't forget your sunglasses!

BOARD INGREDIENTS

1 pineapple

4 oz. whipped cream cheese

½ cup whipped cream

¼ cup powdered sugar

¼ tsp. blue spirulina or 2 drops blue food coloring

12 graham crackers

1 cantaloupe, cubed

1 honeydew, cubed

1 kiwi, peeled and sliced

2 cups watermelon, cubed

2 cups strawberries, rinsed, dried, and sliced

6 Teddy Grahams, plus more for dipping

2 peach ring candies

1 fruit roll-up, cut into 4 pieces

BOARD DIRECTIONS

Start your pool party board by cutting a pineapple in half lengthwise, leaving the top greenery intact. With a knife, carefully remove the inside fruit, making a hollowed-out space for the pool to hold your dip. Cut the fruit into cubes. Place the pineapple shell on the board with the green crown at the top of the board.

Mix together the cream cheese, whipped cream, powdered sugar, and blue tint, and place it inside the pineapple cavity. Using your hands or a rolling pin, crush the graham crackers in a sealed ziplock bag. Spread your sweet sand across the bottom of your board, making a level beach scene. Spread the fruit randomly around the top of the pineapple.

Place your Teddy Grahams upright in the dip as if floating in a peach ring inner tube, or lay them out on fruit roll-up towels. Serve with additional Teddy Grahams for dipping.

BLUEBERRY BREAKFAST
BUFFET

Mornings are important, and our Blueberry Breakfast board celebrates the art of starting the day right, with a harmonious combination of farm-fresh ingredients. The star of the show is the plump fresh blueberries that you can find on the board, as well as in the pancakes, compound butter, and blueberry syrup. To offset the sweetness, we always add in sausage links and simple egg cups. After this breakfast, you can handle anything the day throws at you.

BOARD DIRECTIONS

To prepare the components of this board, first start the Egg and Cheese Cups. While those are in the oven, prepare the compound butter and set it to chill in the fridge. Then cook and cool the Blueberry Syrup. Finally, prepare the pancakes, French toast sticks, and sausages according to package directions.

Just before serving, place small pitchers of your two syrups on the board (the cream server from a tea set works well). Add the compound butter and blueberries, leaving room for the warm food. Then arrange the pancakes, French toast, egg cups, and sausage links. Finally, drizzle a small amount of blueberry syrup over the French toast and sprinkle with powdered sugar.

BOARD INGREDIENTS

5 Egg and Cheese Cups
  (recipe follows)
Blueberry Syrup *(recipe follows)*
Blueberry Compound Butter
  (recipe follows)
5 mini blueberry pancakes
5 French toast sticks
5 sausage links
½ cup maple syrup
2 cups blueberries, rinsed and
  dried
2 tsp. powdered sugar

EGG AND CHEESE CUPS

INGREDIENTS

5 eggs
1¼ cups shredded cheddar cheese
Salt and pepper, to taste
Favorite herbs, preferably fresh

DIRECTIONS

Preheat oven to 350°F. Spray five cups of a six-cup muffin tin with cooking spray. Into each of the five sprayed cups, add one beaten egg, ¼ cup shredded cheese, salt, pepper, and your favorite fresh herbs. Bake for 22 minutes.

YIELD: 5 EGG CUPS

BLUEBERRY SYRUP

INGREDIENTS

1 cup blueberries
1 cup sugar

DIRECTIONS

In a small saucepan over low heat, combine ingredients and stir constantly until sugar has dissolved and berries have softened. Remove from heat and let sit for 10 minutes before serving.

YIELD: 1 CUP

BLUEBERRY COMPOUND BUTTER

DIRECTIONS

In a medium bowl, gently smash blueberries with a fork to release some of the juices. Add butter and sugar, mixing until combined. Refrigerate for 20 minutes to allow it to set up. Serve over warm pancakes and French toast.

YIELD: 4 OUNCES

INGREDIENTS

¼ cup blueberries

1 stick butter, softened

¼ cup powdered sugar

KC BBQ BEEF

Kansas City, my hometown, is known worldwide for our barbeque. Whether on the back patio, in the local BBQ competitions, or in line for the food trucks, everyone is focused on the pork cuts of meat. However, we occasionally just want beef. The beauty of a BBQ beef board is that you can focus on one or two recipes and gather the other offerings from your favorite smokehouse. Ribs are one of our favorite selections to smoke here at the Grace-Filled Homestead. We also love making our own Outlaw Beef Brisket and have shared that recipe in my Grace-Filled Homestead Cookbook. It's fun to cut the brisket into chunks instead of full slices when serving it on a board. We have a favorite local spot across town to source our burnt ends and sirloin. The difference between the burnt ends and the brisket chunks is that the burnt ends come from the naturally fatty pointed end or tip of the brisket. The ends cook down crispy and are so delicious. Let's build this beef board!

BOARD INGREDIENTS

Smoked Beef Ribs
(recipe follows)

½ cup vinegar-based BBQ sauce

½ cup sweet BBQ sauce

1 lb. beef burnt ends

1 lb. grass-fed beef sirloin, sliced

1 lb. Outlaw Beef Brisket Bites
(recipe follows)

BOARD DIRECTIONS

Assemble your board by placing the ribs down the middle and your two sauces at each end. Don't even try to convince anyone that your sauce is better. Those arguments can get heated. Finally, add your burnt ends, sirloin slices, and brisket bites. It's good to let the meat sit for a few minutes before your guests dig in. You can cover the board with foil for up to 30 minutes to keep the food warm while you wait to share the board. This can be a stand-alone board of shareable small bites, or it can be the main event of a meal served with sides.

SMOKED BEEF RIBS

INGREDIENTS

1 (4 lb.) rack beef ribs

1 T. olive oil

½ cup Outlaw BBQ Rub
  (recipe follows)

1 cup apple juice, plus extra for
  spraying every hour

1 cup BBQ sauce (your choice)

DIRECTIONS

Preheat the smoker to 225°F. Loosen the silver membrane from the ribs with a butter knife, tear it off, and discard. Brush room temperature ribs with the olive oil, and cover generously with the Outlaw BBQ Rub. Spray ribs with the apple juice and place them bone side down on the smoker and smoke for 3 hours, spraying apple juice every hour to keep them moist. Remove and wrap the ribs in a double layer of foil and smoke for an additional 2½ hours, maintaining the temperature between 200°F and 250°F. Remove from foil and brush with BBQ sauce. Place meat bone side down on the smoker and smoke for an additional hour. Let ribs rest for 15 minutes before serving.

YIELD: 8 INDIVIDUAL RIBS

OUTLAW BBQ RUB

INGREDIENTS

1 T. cayenne pepper

3 T. smoked paprika

2 T. salt

2 tsp. garlic powder

1 tsp. mustard powder

1 tsp. onion powder

2 tsp. black pepper

½ cup brown sugar

DIRECTIONS

Combine all the ingredients and mix well. The barbecue rub will keep for up to three months stored in a cool, dry place.

YIELD: 10 SERVINGS

OUTLAW BEEF BRISKET BITES

DIRECTIONS

Preheat smoker to 225°F. Place fat side down and remove the thin, silver membrane. Turn over the brisket and trim the fat down to ¼ inch. Coat the entire brisket with the dry rub, working it in generously. Place meat fat side up on the smoker, unwrapped. Smoke until internal temperature reaches 160°F (approximately 8 hours). Roll out a double thick piece of foil and place meat on foil. Spray a generous amount of apple juice on the meat and then tightly wrap. Place brisket back on the smoker until internal temperature reaches 202°F (approximately 2 to 3 hours). Pull meat off the smoker and wrap the foil-wrapped brisket in a towel. Place it in a room temperature cooler to rest for 2 hours. This will keep it warm and allow the juices to settle. Pull brisket out of cooler, unwrap, and slice into bite-size chunks for a charcuterie board, or slice against the grain for a main course. Serve with your favorite sauce. Enjoy!

YIELD: 12 SERVINGS

INGREDIENTS

1 (12 lb.) prime beef brisket, untrimmed

1 cup apple juice

Dipping sauce, for serving

½ cup Outlaw BBQ Rub
(see page 70)

PEACHES AND CREAM BURRATA

Burrata boards are the new trendy foodie dish, and when pairing the creamy goodness with peaches, the fresh summer flavors burst in your mouth. Burrata is similar to mozzarella, yet it has a decadent creamy center that is delicious with sweet fruit as well as savory artichokes and crusty bread.

BOARD DIRECTIONS

Place the burrata in the center of your board. Drain both the peaches and artichokes, placing an artichoke on top of each slice of fruit, and then spacing them out on the board; add pickled onions to the top. Situate the honeycomb and crunchy bread rounds on the board, garnishing with edible flowers and fresh mint. This beautiful and tasty treat refreshes all the senses. Enjoy!

BOARD INGREDIENTS

2 (4 oz.) rounds burrata cheese

1 cup peaches, canned in sweet syrup

1 cup artichoke hearts, marinated in olive oil

½ cup pickled onions

1 honeycomb square

2 cups bruschetta rounds

Edible flowers, for garnish

Mint, for garnish

ONE-POT LOBSTER BOIL

A one-pot lobster boil board is a wonderful way to feed a gathering of friends or family. It makes for a beautiful table display since your food is the centerpiece, as it should be. The scrumptious Lemon Butter is the perfect addition to this board full of goodness!

BOARD INGREDIENTS

1 T. salt

6 oz. Old Bay seasoning

12 red potatoes

2 fresh lobsters, 1 to 2 lbs. each

3 ears corn, each shucked and cut into 3 pieces

½ cup Lemon Butter (recipe follows)

1 lb. jumbo shrimp, deveined

1 lb. smoked sausage, cut into 1-inch pieces

3 lemons, cut in half

BOARD DIRECTIONS

Fill a large stockpot with water, salt, and Old Bay seasoning; bring to a rolling boil. Add in the potatoes and let cook for 8 minutes. While the potatoes are cooking, carefully remove bands from the lobster claws. While the water is still boiling, add the lobster in with the potatoes, head-side down. Cover and cook for approximately 5 minutes. Add in the corn and continue cooking at a simmer for another 5 minutes. Finally, add the shrimp and sausage to the stockpot, cooking for an additional 3 minutes. The lobster should be red and the shrimp pink.

Meanwhile, prepare the Lemon Butter and place a dish of this melted in the center of your board. Drain the stockpot and place all items on the board. Sprinkle a bit more Old Bay seasoning across the board and add in lemon halves.

LEMON BUTTER

INGREDIENTS

½ cup butter, melted

1 tsp. minced garlic

Juice and zest from 1 lemon

Old Bay seasoning (optional)

DIRECTIONS

In a small bowl combine the melted butter, garlic, and lemon juice. Whisk together and then add the lemon zest. Sprinkle in Old Bay seasoning if desired.

YIELD: ½ CUP

ICE CREAM SUNDAE SOCIAL

The ice cream sundae social isn't just a favorite vintage dessert, it's an invitation to savor the simple joys of summer. It's a celebration of the season's abundance and a reminder that life is sweet when shared with those you love. Prepare to indulge in a medley of flavors that will leave your taste buds singing with delight. You can make your own homemade ice cream like our grandparents did, or you can purchase the creamy goodness from the market. Remember, this is a no-guilt zone, and all life hacks are welcome.

BOARD DIRECTIONS

To assemble the board, set out three separate bowls for your three ice cream flavors. Add in three small bowls, one with sprinkles, one with caramel syrup, and one with chocolate syrup. Next, nestle in the sugar cones, brownies, wafer cookies, banana slices, and nuts. Don't forget the favorite toppings of whipped cream and cherries for the top. Just before you serve, scoop the ice cream into the serving bowls.

Although it can get messy, let the little ones make their own masterpiece sundae. They will be beaming with pride as they enjoy their ice cream.

BOARD INGREDIENTS

3 cups vanilla ice cream

3 cups chocolate ice cream

3 cups strawberry ice cream

½ cup rainbow sprinkles

½ cup caramel syrup

½ cup chocolate syrup

6 sugar cones

6 brownies

6 rolled crème filled wafer cookies (we use Pepperidge Farm Pirouettes)

1 banana, sliced in rounds

½ cup nuts (we love cashews on ours)

1 cup whipped cream

½ cup maraschino cherries

THE G.O.A.T. CHEESE WITH STRAWBERRY JALAPEÑO JAM

We love to mix sweet with spicy at the Grace-Filled Homestead. The sweet strawberry season here begins in June. It doesn't last long, so while we can, we like to eat the juicy red treats fresh off the plant, make jam, and add them to every dish we can imagine.

Like the trendy butter boards, the creamy smears of soft cheeses are a delight most can't resist. This board is simple, and it is filled with just the right amount of spice and heat. Candied jalapeños are one of our favorite unique treats here at the Grace-Filled Homestead. . .so hats off to this one, Cowboy.

BOARD DIRECTIONS

To prepare the components of this board, first use the back of your spoon to smear room-temperature goat cheese onto your board in flower petal shapes. Spoon the jam in circles as the center of the flowers. Layer the Cowboy Candy at the bottom of the board, while slicing a few pieces to place as the flower stems. Arrange your cheesecake cups and strawberries, adding the pretzel sticks on the side. If your guests love the sweet and spicy combination, encourage them to top the cheesecake cups with a slice of Cowboy Candy.

BOARD INGREDIENTS

4 oz. goat cheese

Cowboy Candy
(recipe follows)

¼ cup Strawberry Jalapeño Jam
(recipe follows)

10 Strawberry Cheesecake Cups
(recipe follows)

2 cups strawberries

2 cups pretzel sticks

STRAWBERRY JALAPEÑO JAM

DIRECTIONS

Place the strawberries, jalapeños, lemon juice, and pectin into a large saucepan and bring to a full boil over high heat. Once boiling, stir in the sugar until it is dissolved, return the jam to a full boil, and cook for 1 minute. Use a ladle to pour the hot jam into prepared jars and cover tightly with lids. Allow the jam to sit at room temperature for 24 hours to set, then refrigerate for up to a month.

INGREDIENTS

2 cups strawberries, hulled and crushed

½ cup minced jalapeño peppers

⅛ cup lemon juice

3 T. powdered fruit pectin

3½ cups white sugar

2 pint-size glass canning jars with lids, sterilized

YIELD: 4 CUPS

STRAWBERRY CHEESECAKE CUPS

INGREDIENTS

4 oz. goat cheese

¼ cup powdered sugar

10 phyllo shells (pre-baked, thawed if frozen)

Strawberry slices, for serving

DIRECTIONS

In a small bowl, using a hand mixer, whip the goat cheese with the powdered sugar until smooth. Add a small dollop of the mixture to the center of each phyllo shell. Top each with a slice of strawberry.

YIELD: 10 CHEESECAKE CUPS

COWBOY CANDY

DIRECTIONS

Rinse, dry, and slice peppers into ¼-inch-thick rounds. You can remove seeds or leave them in, as preferred. In a medium saucepan, add all the other ingredients and bring to a boil. Reduce the heat to a gentle simmer for 5 minutes. Add in the sliced jalapeños, bring the heat back up to high, and boil for 4 minutes. Using a slotted spoon, evenly transfer only the peppers to prepared jars, leaving ½ inch of headspace at the top. Boil the liquid for another 6 to 7 minutes. Remove the pan from heat and let mixture cool for about 3 minutes. Using a ladle, pour the liquid syrup into the jars, making sure all the jalapeños are completely submerged. Seal, place in the fridge, and eat within 2 months.

YIELD: 2 CUPS

INGREDIENTS

10 jalapeños

1 cup apple cider vinegar

1 cup sugar

1 cup brown sugar, packed

½ tsp. turmeric

½ tsp. garlic powder

½ tsp. cayenne pepper

2 half-pint glass canning jars with lids, sterilized

FALL

As summer begins to fade into the golden glow of autumn, the Grace-Filled Homestead comes alive with a renewed sense of abundance and tranquility. Fall descends upon the farm with a gentle crispness in the air as the kitchen is filled with canning supplies and harvested produce. The small orchard on our property bursts with ripe apples and a variety of pumpkins, inviting us to partake in the joyous harvest season. The changing landscape is a canvas of colored leaves, signaling the time for cozy gatherings and hearty feasts that begin with a beautiful board.

So many of our boards are enjoyed outdoors. We love the simplicity and beauty of an outdoor gathering under twinkle lights. The casual atmosphere invites long conversations and true connections with loved ones over a few bites of cheese or sweets. After a long day of harvesting and cleaning up the gardens, fall evenings beckon us to gather around firepits and sip on steaming cups of apple cider or cocoa. The Campfire Candy S'mores board is a wonderful way to transport all the ingredients to your sweet activity. Fall is pumpkin spice season, and the baked brie and spiced treats on the Brie Bites and Autumn Spice board fill the air with comforting aromas, creating a delicious symphony of flavors.

Within this chapter, you'll discover an array of charcuterie boards designed to complement the enchanting spirit of fall. From the Game Day board to the sophisticated Individual Caprese Minis and the indulgent Maple Pecan Butter Board, each creation is a testament to the beauty of the season. As fall progresses, we look forward to the grand culmination of the season—Thanksgiving. It's a time for gratitude and gathering with our favorite people. Our fall boards bring people together. Join us in embracing the charm of autumn. It's a celebration of fall's bounty and the warmth that permeates our homes during this cherished time of year.

The changing landscape is a canvas of colored leaves, signaling the time for cozy gatherings and hearty feasts that begin with a beautiful board.

BOARD ESSENTIALS FOR ANYTIME HOSPITALITY

In any home, the heart of hospitality expands in moments of connection. There's a unique charm to impromptu gatherings and last-minute dinners and the spontaneity of shared experiences, laughter, and, of course, the culinary delights that bring everyone together. At the Grace-Filled Homestead, we've discovered that having a well-stocked pantry and refrigerator can turn an in-the-moment gathering into a memorable feast, especially when a delightful charcuterie board is the centerpiece.

Hospitality is a timeless art, and the joy of sharing food is magnified when it's unexpected and happens without the stress and perfectionism that can come with a planned event. When a neighbor unexpectedly drops by or a nearby family loses their power after a storm, welcoming them into your home and creating a board filled with their favorite snacks will make them feel treasured. Often, the reason someone stops by unannounced is because they are having a bad day and need comfort or cheer. I know from experience that it feels like pure magic when a chaotic situation is transformed with cozy and calming nourishment that lets a guest know you are eager to help and support them. People feel special when you open your doors and hearts to them, offering a spread that shows they're valued and cherished.

To elevate any impromptu gathering, having a thoughtfully stocked pantry is essential. At the Grace-Filled Homestead, our pantry is always armed with key ingredients for a stellar charcuterie board. Green olives and kalamata olives provide a savory burst, while stone-ground mustard adds a zesty kick. For a touch of sweetness, add fig jam, dried fruit, and honey roasted cashews to create a harmonious balance that delights the palate. These pantry staples effortlessly come together to form the foundation of an exquisite charcuterie experience.

A well-curated charcuterie board is incomplete without a selection of cheeses, and our refrigerator stores an array of them. Goat cheese, our favorite, offers a creamy texture; cheddar provides a sharp bite; Gruyère adds a nutty richness. The trio creates a diverse flavor profile that caters to various preferences. For the meat lovers, a stash of pepperoni and sausage rolls adds a savory dimension, ensuring there's something for every palate. Of course, we always have a few varieties of crackers in the house. The salty crunch of a cracker is the building block for a customized bite of goodness.

In the hustle and bustle of daily life, the ability to whip up a stunning charcuterie board on a moment's notice—and make people feel not only welcome but truly cherished—is a testament to the art of gracious living. At the Grace-Filled Homestead, we believe that these impromptu gatherings, complete with a thoughtfully crafted board, are the moments that define and elevate the spirit of hospitality.

So, the next time an unexpected knock on the door turns into a gathering of friends or family, rest assured that your stocked refrigerator and pantry will have all you need to transform the ordinary into the extraordinary and create warm memories, satisfy taste buds, and fulfill hearts.

STOCK UP ON THESE STAPLES

OLIVES

NUTS

PICKLED VEGGIES

CRACKERS OF SEVERAL VARIETIES

HONEY

STONE-GROUND MUSTARD

FIG JAM

DRIED FRUIT

CHEESE

CURED MEATS

Share with the Lord's people who are in need. Practice hospitality.

Romans 12:13

AFTER-SCHOOL YES SNACKS

Back-to-school season can be stressful for both parents and kiddos. Days filled with academics and extracurricular activities need to be fueled with healthy and fun snacks. We call this our simple Yes Snacks board, which basically tells the kids, "You can have anything on this board, but don't go scavenging through the kitchen and ruining your dinner." We fill the board with a few fruits and veggies, cheese, and even sandwich bites. It's enough to keep their energy up during play and study time, but it also leaves room for a family dinner.

BOARD DIRECTIONS

To assemble the Yes board, we first cut our sandwich into quarters and place it on the board. Then we add the fruits and veggies. We love the thick, shorter pretzel sticks, and we place them next to the grapes. Finally, we use our small star cookie cutter to make stars from the sliced cheese. This simple step is what makes this tray so extra fun.

BOARD INGREDIENTS

1 peanut butter sandwich

1 cluster grapes

8 strawberries

12 sugar snap peas

12 pretzel sticks

2 slices Colby-Jack cheese

INDIVIDUAL CAPRESE MINIS

Sometimes we don't want to share! Overall, the concept of charcuterie boards and entertaining spreads is all about sharing, grazing together, and interacting with others. However, sometimes we can push back on that idea and keep all the goodness to ourselves. Individual mini boards like this one became popular during the pandemic, and now they have become a favorite indulgence. We've seen them served at corporate events as team members are heading into a long meeting. They've been offered as a first appetizer or salad course at a sit-down meal, or they've been a grab-and-mingle starter at a social event. We love this idea and the cute little boards that go with it. Start with four mini boards and enjoy our take on the classic caprese salad.

BOARD INGREDIENTS

4 slices French bread
2 T. butter
2 T. olive oil
1 T. Italian seasoning blend
4 sprigs fresh basil
4 slices heirloom tomato
4 slices mozzarella
4 T. balsamic glaze
Coarse salt (optional)

BOARD DIRECTIONS

Preheat oven to 400°F. Butter each slice of French bread and toast in your preheated oven for 3 minutes, flip over, and toast for an additional 3 minutes. Remove from the oven, drizzle with olive oil, and sprinkle Italian seasoning on top. To assemble the individual boards, simply place the basil down first, layering the tomato and cheese slices next. Finish off with one piece of toast for each board and drizzle balsamic glaze over the entire spread. You can sprinkle coarse flaky salt if you desire. We serve the boards with a small decorative fork, but fingers are also acceptable with individual boards. Enjoy!

FROMAGE AND FIGS

A fig and cheese board is one of the simplest yet most delicious boards you can serve. All flavors of fromage can elevate your next gathering by combining them on a board with a scrumptious seasonal jam. Whenever we share a simple cheese board, we do splurge on the flavors and find some rare combinations, but ease is key here. Let your own preferences and the size of your crowd determine how much you serve of each item.

BOARD DIRECTIONS

Place the Fig Jam in a small dish in the corner of your board. Make sure you have a small serving spoon and a few cheese knives nearby. Cut your figs in half lengthwise, and spread the fruit pieces across the board. Fill in the additional space with the four wedges of cheese, slicing off 2 to 3 pieces for guests to get started with. Serve with crackers or crusty bread.

FIG JAM

DIRECTIONS

Cut figs into ½-inch pieces. Place in a small saucepan over medium heat. Add the sugar and stir continuously for 5 minutes, coating the figs completely and allowing the sugar to dissolve in the juices. Add the lemon juice and water and bring the mixture to a boil. Stir continuously for an additional 5 minutes. Reduce heat to low and simmer, stirring continuously until the mixture thickens to your desired consistency, about 15 minutes. Spoon into a serving dish and allow to cool.

YIELD: 1 CUP

BOARD INGREDIENTS

Fig Jam
  (recipe follows)
Fresh figs
Rosemary Asiago wedge
Gouda wedge
BellaVitano cabernet sauvignon
  wedge
Pepper Gruyère wedge
Crackers or crusty bread

INGREDIENTS

4 figs, stems removed
⅓ cup sugar
Juice of 1 lemon
2 T. water

SWEET HONEYCOMB, MEAT, AND CHEESE CHARCUTERIE

Honey is often found on charcuterie boards. The sweet nectar offsets the savory taste of cured meats and aged cheeses. Serving it in its natural honeycomb form adds texture, earthy flavors, and beauty. A traditional charcuterie board has meat and cheese elements as well as nuts, olives, and fruit. The meat roses take this traditional board to the next level.

BOARD INGREDIENTS

Honeycomb

4 slices prosciutto

8 slices salami

3 meat roses
(see page 141)

4 slices Asiago

4 slices sharp cheddar

4 slices Gruyère

½ cup green olives

½ cup kalamata olives

½ cup cashews

Bruschetta rounds

2 figs

BOARD DIRECTIONS

To make the honeycomb the center of attention, elevate it on a cupcake stand and place it in the center of the board. Fold the prosciutto and layer it in a corner, adding the salami and the meat roses on separate sides of the tray. Follow the directions for pepperoni roses to make flower-bud shapes. You can use this technique with pepperoni, salami, or similar cured meats, as you choose. Arrange and place the cheeses across from each other, filling in the smaller spaces with olives, nuts, and bruschetta rounds. The last step is to slice the figs and nestle them in the open spaces.

GAME DAY CHEESE BALL

Whether you're tailgating in a parking lot or hosting a game day gathering at home, the Game Day Cheese Ball board is a testament to the abundance of the fall season, promising a touchdown of joy for all who gather around. We take our football seriously here at the Grace-Filled Homestead and choose to celebrate with friends and family regularly to cheer on our hometown team.

The cheese ball, shaped like a football, is coated in savory bacon. It becomes the star player on a board surrounded by a lineup of buffalo wings, mini sweet peppers, crisp celery sticks, fresh broccoli florets, and sugar snap peas.

BOARD DIRECTIONS

Place the cheese ball in the center of your board. Rinse and dry all your vegetables. Chop the broccoli into bite-size pieces, and cut the celery into 2-inch pieces. Position all the veggies on the board, and add your crackers next to the cheese ball. Finally, warm buffalo wings and your favorite dipping sauce can be added just before serving.

BOARD INGREDIENTS

2 cups broccoli florets

6 celery ribs

2 cups mini sweet peppers

1 cup sugar snap peas

20 crackers

Football Cheese Ball
(recipe follows)

2 dozen prepared buffalo wings
(your favorite recipe)

Ranch or blue cheese
dipping sauce

FOOTBALL CHEESE BALL

DIRECTIONS

Combine cream cheese, spices, and hot sauce, stirring together until smooth. Add 1 cup bacon and the jalapeños, green onions, and Colby-Jack cheese. Let the mixture rest in the refrigerator for 2 hours to set up. Scoop the cheese mixture out onto a long piece of plastic wrap. Spray your hands with cooking spray, and then mold the cheese mixture into a football shape with a flat base. Tightly wrap the cheese ball with the plastic wrap so it can hold its shape. Refrigerate for 4 hours. Unwrap the cheese ball and carefully roll it in the remaining chopped bacon, pressing the pieces in. Slice the provolone into inch-long rectangles and place them on top of the football to create the laces.

INGREDIENTS

16 oz. cream cheese, softened

1 T. Cajun seasoning

1 tsp. cumin

1 T. garlic salt

1 tsp. smoked paprika

1 tsp. red pepper flakes

1 tsp. hot sauce

2 cups chopped cooked bacon,
divided

¼ cup diced jalapeños

¼ cup chopped green onions

2 cups shredded Colby-Jack
cheese

2 slices provolone cheese

YIELD: 10 SERVINGS

MAPLE PECAN BUTTER BOARD

This fall-inspired acorn-shaped board is adorned with an array of creamy farm-fresh ingredients, each thoughtfully chosen to bring warmth and joy to your gatherings. At the heart of this masterpiece lies a velvety canvas of sweet cream butter. We've generously swirled in Nutella, adding a luscious chocolate-hazelnut dimension that pairs beautifully with the buttery base. To introduce a delightful crunch, we've scattered finely chopped pecans, a nod to the bountiful harvest of the season.

What truly elevates this rich centerpiece is the drizzle of pure maple syrup that cascades over the ensemble, infusing every bite with a sweet and autumnal essence.

BOARD INGREDIENTS

1 stick butter, softened

3 T. Nutella

½ cup honey roasted pecans, chopped

3 T. maple syrup

Bread or crackers for dipping

BOARD DIRECTIONS

Spread softened butter across the board with the back of a spoon, leaving visible 2-inch strokes to keep some texture and interest. On top of the butter add warmed Nutella in six evenly spaced dollops, spreading it out across the butter. Next, sprinkle the board with the chopped pecans, and drizzle the maple syrup on top. Serve with your favorite breads or crackers to enjoy the creamy goodness.

CAMPFIRE CANDY S'MORES

As the autumn air turns crisp, it's time to head outside, light the camp-fire, and make s'mores. Our s'mores board has all the standard basic ingredients we love, but we also add in some additional candy choices such as peanut butter cups, KitKats, and Cherry Mash. If you love sweet and gooey s'mores but are not a fan of the sticky mess, the alternative S'mores Crunchy Campfire Cones recipe is for you. It has all the melted goodness of s'mores contained in a crunchy sugar cone. Button up your flannel shirt, light the fire, and get ready for some fun! Don't forget your campfire stories.

BOARD DIRECTIONS

After you light your campfire outside, let it develop some coals. Set out long roasting sticks so your guests can toast their marshmallow to their own preference. Place marshmallows on a tray and surround them with the various chocolate candies, graham cracker squares and the ingredients for yummy S'mores Chocolate Peanut Butter Cones. Let your guests build, roast, and enjoy their own personalized s'more.

BOARD INGREDIENTS

4 cups large marshmallows
8 snack size (½ oz.) chocolate bars
8 snack size (½ oz.) KitKats
8 Cherry Mash
8 chocolate peanut butter cups
18 graham cracker squares
S'mores Chocolate Peanut Butter
  Cones *(recipe follows)*

S'MORES CHOCOLATE PEANUT BUTTER CONES

DIRECTIONS

Light your campfire outside and place a grate a couple of inches above the flames. Lay out six sugar cones on a tray. Break graham crackers into smaller pieces, but don't overwork them into a powder. In each sugar cone, add layers of marshmallows, graham cracker pieces, and chocolate chips or Reese's Pieces (or both!). Repeat the layers until the cone is three-fourths full. Wrap each cone with foil and place it on the grate above the fire. Allow it to cook above the flames for about 3 to 5 minutes. Use barbecue tongs to remove the cones from the fire. Be careful when removing the foil—don't burn yourself!

INGREDIENTS

6 sugar ice cream cones
6 graham crackers
1½ cups mini marshmallows
1½ cups chocolate chips
1 cup Reese's Pieces

YIELD: 6 SERVINGS

BRIE BITES AND AUTUMN SPICE

At the heart of this board are the Brie Puff Pastry Pumpkins, filled with creamy decadence and wrapped in layers of flaky perfection. To complement these Brie Bites, we've added pumpkin spiced bread, apple and pecan pies, and crunchy candied pecans. Each bite is a harmonious blend of cinnamon, nutmeg, and autumn goodness.

BOARD INGREDIENTS

1 mini apple pie

2 mini pecan pies

6 slices pumpkin spiced bread

1 cup candied pecans

6 slices of pepper jack cheese
(3 oz. total)

2 Brie Puff Pastry Pumpkins
(recipe follows)

BOARD DIRECTIONS

Before assembling this board, I start with a trip to my local bakery and farmers market, looking for the fall-flavored mini pies, pumpkin bread, and candied nuts. Once I'm stocked up on my favorite fall sweets, I start making the savory Brie Puff Pastry Pumpkins recipe. While they are in the oven, carefully place the cheese slices, pies, and sliced bread on the board, filling in areas with the pecans. Finally, add the pastry pumpkins and enjoy with your favorite people.

BRIE PUFF PASTRY PUMPKINS

INGREDIENTS

1 puff pastry sheet

2 T. flour for surface prep

4 T. pumpkin butter

4 mini brie wheels (approximately
1 oz. each)

Baker's twine

1 egg

4 sage leaves

4 pretzel sticks

DIRECTIONS

Preheat oven to 375°F. Lay the puff pastry on a floured surface and divide into four squares. Spread a spoonful of pumpkin butter in the middle of each. Place a mini wheel of brie cheese on top of the pumpkin butter. Wrap the puff pastry around the cheese and pinch to seal. Tie baker's twine at even intervals around the brie to make the pumpkin indentions. Whisk the egg and brush it over the puff pastry. Place pastry on an ungreased baking sheet. Bake for 20 minutes. Let cool for 10 minutes, then carefully cut and remove the baker's twine, and add sage leaves and pretzels on top for the pumpkin stem and leaf.

YIELD: 4 SERVINGS

HARVEST BLESSINGS
CORNUCOPIA

This Thanksgiving cornucopia spread displays the bountiful blessings of the season and farm-fresh goodness. This harvest-inspired creation is a freshly baked, golden-brown cornucopia bread bowl. The edible horn of plenty is overflowing with the finest offerings of fruits, nuts, vegetables, artisanal cheeses, and savory cured meats.

BOARD DIRECTIONS

Place your prepared Thanksgiving Cornucopia on the back corner of the board. Cut one of the pomegranates in half, adding one full pomegranate to one corner of the board and the two halves on opposite sides. Place the fruits and veggies so they are pouring out of the cornucopia. Set a small bowl filled with the ranch dip nearby. Then add the meat, cheese, and nuts to your board. Remind your guests that the cornucopia is a pull-apart bread to snack on.

BOARD INGREDIENTS

Thanksgiving Cornucopia
  (recipe follows)

2 pomegranates

½ cup Sugared Cranberries
  (recipe follows)

2 clusters of grapes, rinsed
  and dried

2 cups cauliflower, rinsed, dried,
  and cut into bite-size pieces

2 cups broccoli, rinsed, dried, and
  cut into bite-size pieces

½ cup ranch dip

12 slices salami

Asiago cheese wedge

1 cup mixed nuts

THANKSGIVING CORNUCOPIA

INGREDIENTS

2 T. flour for surface prep
1 (16 oz.) ball pizza dough
1 egg, beaten

DIRECTIONS

Preheat oven to 400°F. Roll a solid cone of foil that will serve as a mold for the cornucopia; bend the end up for the cornucopia shape. Coat the exterior with cooking spray. Roll out the pizza dough on a floured board, cut long strips of dough about 1 inch wide, and wrap the strips around the foil cone, covering the entire surface. Braid the final three strips and place them around the opening. Secure all pieces with an egg wash and brush a final coat of egg over the entire cone. Bake for 8 minutes. Let it cool completely, and carefully remove all or most of the foil cone. (I leave the tail foil pieces in to avoid breakage.) Place your cornucopia on a large board and fill the center with your favorite meats, cheeses, fruits, veggies, nuts, and dips.

YIELD: 12 SERVINGS

SUGARED CRANBERRIES

DIRECTIONS

Dip the cranberries in warmed maple syrup and place them on a piece of parchment paper to set for 1 minute. Then roll the cranberries in sugar and leave them to dry for 30 minutes.

YIELD: 1 CUP

INGREDIENTS

1 cup fresh cranberries
3 T. maple syrup
Granulated sugar, for rolling

VEGGIE-TURKEY CRUDITÉ

Toby the Turkey is the unofficial boss of our feisty flock at the Grace-Filled Homestead. He is handsome and knows he is a part of the family and will never be served at a holiday meal. Even Toby can feel good about this turkey crudité board at your Thanksgiving celebration. This healthy option will have your family members happy to be snacking on all the fresh vegetables.

BOARD INGREDIENTS

5 celery ribs

3 carrots

1 cup cauliflower florets

1 cup broccoli florets

1 cucumber, sliced

1 cup ranch dip

1 orange bell pepper

1 black olive

2 mini sweet peppers, yellow and red

BOARD DIRECTIONS

Rinse and dry all vegetables. Cut the celery and carrots into 3-inch sticks and arrange them in an arch. Add the cauliflower, broccoli, and cucumbers also in the arch shape. This forms the turkey's spread tail feathers. Add a bowl of dip just below the arch. Cut the bottom off the bell pepper and place upside down in the dip for the turkey head. Slice the olive and place two pieces for the eyes. Cut the mini peppers and form small pieces into the shape of a beak and a snood and place them on the head. Finally, cut one of the carrot sticks in half and notch out the bottom for the turkey legs, placing them on the dip.

WINTER

Winter descends upon the Grace-Filled Homestead like a blanket of soft snow, transforming the landscape into a magical wonderland. As the hills are covered in a glistening white coat and the air turns crisp, our hearts warm in anticipation of the joyous season ahead. We welcome winter with open arms, embracing the traditions and festivities that come with this enchanting time of year.

In the winter chapter of our charcuterie journey, we find ourselves immersed in celebrating the birth of our Savior, ringing in the new year, and expressing love for our sweethearts. Family and friends gather around, creating memories that will be cherished for years to come. The Movie Night Concessions and Sushi Spread offerings are perfect for a cozy night spent gathered around the fireplace.

The winter homestead is adorned with vintage Christmas decor, grandma's nativity scene, and twinkling lights that illuminate both house and tree. Every moment is a celebration of winter's magic, from the thrill of sledding down snow-covered slopes, to a comforting Hot Cocoa Station on a chilly evening, to the exchange of thoughtful gifts that reflect the love and care of the holidays. And when work parties add merriment to your season's schedule, celebrate friends and coworkers with a carefully crafted charcuterie board.

As we assemble gift-box boards for our neighbors, usher in the new year with sparkling festivities, and enjoy chocolate-covered strawberries with our favorite valentines, the charcuterie board becomes a versatile canvas for creating culinary masterpieces that enhance the joyous occasion. Don't forget the chocolate-covered bacon. It may be the most favored ingredient on any board in this book.

A cozy, festive spread adds to the joy of any event and reflects the magic of winter on the farm. Each board is a testament to the warmth and connection that winter brings, and we hope these creations become a cherished part of your own seasonal traditions. Let your homestead—whether it is an apartment, a ranch, or a ranch house in the suburbs—be filled with love, laughter, and the delightful flavors of winter.

A cozy, festive spread adds to the joy of any event and reflects the magic of winter.

BEAUTIFUL BOARD BASICS

At the Grace-Filled Homestead, we transform everyday dishes and platters into beautiful boards filled with seasonal garden-fresh spreads. The choice of the board is a key element in this culinary canvas. It can set the tone and dress code for your entire gathering as you bring together neighbors, family, and friends to delight in the feast.

We have rolled out butcher paper for a larger casual spread, and we've brought out Grandma's elegant china plate for an intimate special occasion. When you begin by choosing the right board, the ingredient decision-making is easier.

Of course, wooden charcuterie boards are a common choice and come in all different shapes and sizes. Oak, walnut, and pine are some of our favorite varieties. Two of our boards were made by our sons in woodshop class and another was given to us as a gift from a friend. We also have a few vintage, weathered boards that are extra special because they remind us of the fun day we had when we came across them while antiquing.

One popular choice for charcuterie boards is marble, known for its elegance and timeless appeal. Marble is heavy and makes a substantial foundation for your gathering. It provides a sleek and sophisticated backdrop that is easy to clean up after your gathering.

We love our slate board with a distinct contrast to the white shiny marble. It has a dark and moody vibe with rustic charm. A slate board also serves as a natural chalkboard, allowing for creative labeling of each tasty offering.

Bamboo boards are an excellent choice,

especially if you are looking for an eco-friendly option. Bamboo is not only sustainable but it's lightweight and easy to clean. The natural grain pattern adds an Asian aesthetic to a sushi board.

We also love going vertical with our space-saving boards. Tiered trays and donut walls have a visual impact on your gathering, and they can be a fun centerpiece for your party. Adding in levels allows for more offerings in a small space. You can purchase trays or make your own levels with crates and boxes covered in tablecloths and runners. A new twist to a large grazing tray is an individual charcuterie experience. We have some tiny wooden boards that allow each guest to have their own. We've also used individual cones and flat-bottomed disposable cups. Many types of these cups and cones are available for purchase. Being able to hold your own charcuterie cup allows you to mingle through the room of a larger gathering.

At the Grace-Filled Homestead, we believe that the artistry of charcuterie starts with the perfect canvas to showcase a beautiful, colorful palette of ingredients. You have so many options, so get creative and have some fun with it. No matter which canvas you choose, you will see the true beauty of the board unfold as it brings together friends, strangers, family members, and all you welcome to the table with a spirit of love and hospitality.

I am beginning to learn that it is the sweet, simple things of life which are the real ones after all.

Laura Ingalls Wilder

CHOCOLATE-COVERED BACON CAPRESE CONES

Is there anything better than chocolate and bacon all in one bite? I think not. This magical addition to your gathering will leave your guests speechless. A charcuterie cone is the perfect way to enjoy a caprese salad on the go, and these individual bites are handheld, eliminating the need for utensils. For preparation, you will want a pipette to help drizzle the balsamic glaze.

BOARD DIRECTIONS

There are many cone display options available to purchase; however, my favorite way to serve Chocolate-Covered Bacon Caprese Cones is by simply turning a wire basket upside down. To assemble, place your cones upright in the slots of the basket. First, add a wrapped chocolate to the bottom of each cone (our favorite are the individually wrapped Lindor truffles). Next, add 1 tablespoon of mixed nuts. Place one slice of chocolate covered bacon inside but sticking up out of the cone. Then make your skewers, alternating the mozzarella and cherry tomatoes on larger sticks. Place them upright in the cones. Add your meat stick, two crackers, a slice of cheddar cheese, one okra pickle, and three olives on a toothpick skewer. Fill the empty pipettes by squeezing the air out and adding the tip into the balsamic glaze, backfilling the pipette with the sweet natural goodness. Add one filled pipette to each cone and garnish with fresh basil.

BOARD INGREDIENTS

12 waffle sugar cones
12 wrapped chocolate truffle balls
¾ cup mixed nuts
Chocolate-Covered Bacon
 (recipe follows)
12 (6 inch) skewers
24 mozzarella pearls
24 cherry tomatoes
12 meat sticks
24 crackers
12 slices cheddar
12 pickled okra
36 green olives
12 toothpicks
12 pipettes
½ cup balsamic glaze
12 sprigs basil

CHOCOLATE-COVERED BACON

DIRECTIONS

Chocolate-covered bacon is always the star of the show. It's important to use thick-cut bacon because it is less fragile. I like to prepare a few extra pieces in case one breaks in the process. Melt chocolate pieces on stovetop on low, preferably in a double boiler, stirring continuously for approximately 3 minutes or until smooth. Immediately remove from heat and carefully dip the bacon into the chocolate, covering the top 2 inches. Carefully place on parchment paper to set for 5 minutes.

YIELD: 15 SLICES

INGREDIENTS

8 oz. chocolate melting wafers
15 slices thick-cut bacon, cooked

SUSHI SPREAD WITH SPICY PEANUT PLUM SAUCE

On a sushi spread, there is something for everyone, even the most hesitant. Many have a misconception that sushi is made with raw seafood, but it doesn't have to be. With this board you can pick and choose your favorite additions, making your own or using carryout selections. This bamboo sushi board can be a complete meal when you include noodles and condiments.

BOARD INGREDIENTS

1 cup edamame, warm
½ tsp. kosher salt flakes
4 seafood spring rolls (purchased)
9 California rolls (purchased)
5 Godzilla rolls (purchased)
5 crunch rolls (purchased)
⅓ cup pickled ginger
3 T. wasabi
1 (4 oz.) can mandarin orange
    slices
1 cucumber, sliced
1 T. everything bagel seasoning
3 cups ramen noodles, prepared
Spicy Peanut Plum Sauce
    (recipe follows)

BOARD DIRECTIONS

Place your warm edamame on a bamboo board, and sprinkle salt over the edamame. Surround it with your various sushi rolls. Assemble the condiments board by displaying the ginger, wasabi, oranges, and cucumber slices. Sprinkle the bagel seasoning over the cucumbers and wasabi. Add the ramen noodles in a bowl and serve with another bowl of Spicy Peanut Plum Sauce.

SPICY PEANUT PLUM SAUCE

INGREDIENTS

½ cup prepared plum sauce
3 T. soy sauce
2 T. peanut butter
1 cup water
1 tsp. smoked paprika

DIRECTIONS

If you are tired of a boring soy sauce, you can take your spread up a notch with this Spicy Peanut Plum Sauce. It has a savory depth with added heat and sweet nutty flavors. Simply combine all ingredients in a small saucepan, stirring over low heat for 5 minutes. Serve warm.

YIELD: 1½ CUPS

ROSEMARY CHARCUTERIE WREATH

Rosemary is a festive herb that looks like an evergreen forest and smells fresh with hints of mint. This board will tantalize all your senses with the holiday flavors, textures, and aromas. Your guests will enjoy a mixture of salty and sweet treats complete with olives, nuts, pepperoni roses, cheeses, chocolate, and fruits such as juicy pomegranates and dried apricots. Welcome your friends and family with this simple and memorable holiday board.

BOARD DIRECTIONS

On a round board, place 9 sprigs of rosemary around the outside edges, and form a small circle in the middle of the board with the remaining 3 herb sprigs. Cut the pomegranates in half, evenly spacing them inside the rosemary-outlined wreath. Next place two small bowls on the board and fill them with olives. Add the pepperoni roses in bunches of three along with three piles of pistachios. Fill in the empty spaces with cheese, fruit, peppermints, and chocolate-covered pretzels.

BOARD INGREDIENTS

12 sprigs fresh rosemary

2 pomegranates

1 cup green olives

1 cup kalamata olives

9 pepperoni roses
   (see page 141)

1½ cups pistachios in the shell

10 cheese slices, such as Colby
   or Monterey Jack

1 cup dried apricots

½ cup Sugared Cranberries
   (see page 109)

1 cup peppermint candies

½ cup chocolate-covered pretzels

CANDY CANE CAPRESE

We love our cheese and tomatoes at the Grace-Filled Homestead. The candy cane–shaped caprese salad is a fun addition to any holiday gathering. You can throw it together in less than 5 minutes, and I promise there will not be anything left within an hour of you setting out the board.

BOARD INGREDIENTS

1 loaf French bread
2 T. butter
2 T. olive oil
2 T. Italian seasoning blend
9 slices heirloom tomato
8 large slices mozzarella
10 sprigs fresh basil
4 T. balsamic glaze

BOARD DIRECTIONS

Preheat the oven to 400°F. First, make crostini by slicing your French bread into serving rounds. Butter each slice and toast in the oven for 3 minutes, then flip them over and toast for an additional 3 minutes. Remove from the oven, drizzle with olive oil, and sprinkle Italian seasoning on top. Begin forming your savory candy cane with a tomato slice to start the curve. Then layer a slice of cheese, alternating until you complete the candy cane shape. Randomly tuck in basil leaves under the tomatoes, and drizzle the balsamic glaze over the top. Pile your crostini bread in the corner and enjoy!

CHARCUTERIE GIFT BOX

This fun and simple charcuterie on the go makes a wonderful hostess gift for your next evening out. It is also a wonderful treat to deliver to your neighbors, coworkers, teachers, and delivery drivers who work so hard throughout the year. This thoughtful box is easy to put together and is always appreciated.

BOARD DIRECTIONS

I like to add parchment paper to the bottom of the box first and then fill in the four corners with the orange, pepperoni roses, brie wheel, and hazelnut truffles. In the middle of the box place the cheddar, crackers, and both types of nuts. Add the peppermint candies, cranberries, candy canes, and rosemary. Add the lid and a bow to make someone feel special.

SUPPLIES

1 holiday-inspired box or tin

BOARD INGREDIENTS

½ orange

4 pepperoni roses
  (see page 141)

1 (8 oz.) brie wheel

4 chocolate hazelnut truffles,
  wrapped

4 slices cheddar

10 crackers

1 cup candied pecans

½ cup pistachios in the shell

6 peppermint candies

½ cup Sugared Cranberries
  (see page 109)

2 candy canes

Rosemary sprigs, for garnish

HOT COCOA STATION

As the temperatures cool down, sipping hot cocoa by the fire is a family tradition. Adding sweet goodies to a tray can make a fun serve-yourself station for your friends and family. Pouring warm milk over powdered cocoa mix brings back memories of all those vintage Christmas decorations and holiday movies. No one needs to know just how many treats you add to your cozy cup of goodness. Just like Christmas, this experience will delight kids of all ages.

BOARD INGREDIENTS

1½ cups powdered cocoa mix

1 cup mini marshmallows

2 cups flavored specialty marshmallows

12 rolled crème filled wafer cookies (we use Pepperidge Farms Pirouttes)

12 powdered sugar dipping cookies

12 peppermint candies

8 cinnamon sticks

1 cup heavy whipping cream

6 crushed peppermint candy stir sticks

6 white chocolate–covered chocolate spoons

8 cups milk

BOARD DIRECTIONS

Place your powdered cocoa mix in a bowl with a serving spoon. Add the marshmallows, cookies, candy, and cinnamon sticks to the board. Add the heavy whipping cream to a pouring dish and fill in the extra spaces with the stirring sticks and chocolate-covered spoons. Set out your favorite holiday mugs. Warm the milk on the stove and serve it in an insulated carafe to pour over the powdered cocoa mix.

YEAR-END REFLECTIONS

As the year comes to a close, it's time to reflect on the past and set goals for the year ahead. Who says a serving board has to be wood or granite? Mirrors make the best boards ever. This chunky mirror is used throughout the season as a candle holder, but on New Year's Eve it makes a beautiful reflective serving tray. The hot honey adds some spice and heat to this board. It's elegant yet simple and can even be used for a party of two.

BOARD DIRECTIONS

Clean the mirror and frame carefully before assembling this board. Cut the figs in half lengthwise and place them in the corners. Add the grapes next to the figs, and fill in the center with the pita rounds, cheese, olives, and nuts. Drizzle the board with spicy hot honey.

BOARD INGREDIENTS

3 figs

3 clusters seedless grapes, rinsed and dried

6 pita bread rounds

4 mini brie wheels (approximately 1 oz. each)

½ cup blue cheese–stuffed olives

½ cup cashews

¼ cup spicy hot honey

NEW YEAR'S SPARKLE DELIGHTS

Toasts to the new year are extra special when centered around a sparkle board. Of course, we offer the traditional bubbly drinks and black-eyed peas for good luck. If you're not already a fan of black-eyed peas, you will be once you add bacon. Only a bite is required for the folklore luck. We've layered in all the fun meats, cheeses, olives, and sweets. Don't forget to light a sparkler for a fun effect.

BOARD INGREDIENTS

1 ice mold suited for a wine chiller

1 bottle sparkling cider (nonalcoholic is just as fun)

2 cups black-eyed peas cooked with real bacon

5 shooter glasses

5 mini white cupcakes with sprinkles

1 cup mixed olives

8 pieces salami

6 slices Gouda cheese

6 slices swiss cheese

12 crackers

20 chocolate gold coins

1 cup white chocolate–covered pretzels

8 pieces white fudge

5 chocolate hazelnut truffles, wrapped

1 sparkler (optional)

BOARD DIRECTIONS

First, use a specialty ice mold to create a cooler for your sparkling wine or cider. Begin by filling the mold with gold curling ribbon. Then fill the container with water and freeze for 4 hours. Run the mold under room-temperature water to unmold. Place your sparkling cider inside the ice container to chill. Spoon your black-eyed peas into shooter glasses and add mini forks, and place them on the board. Add your cupcakes and olive medley next, and then layer in the meat, cheese, crackers, and sweet treats.

Place a sparkler, if desired, in one of the cupcakes and carefully light it, ringing in the new year. As always, supervise the little ones and proceed safely with lighters and sparks.

MOVIE NIGHT CONCESSIONS

Movie nights are a fun tradition at the Grace-Filled Homestead. Whether you are curled up on your couch or outside with a sheet and projector, this board will be a memory maker. It's filled with all the vintage snack favorites, traditional candies, and of course, buttery popcorn. This simple and portable board is all you, your friends, and family will need while watching your favorite box office hit.

BOARD DIRECTIONS

To assemble the board, add your popcorn to the middle with the large lollipop on top. Place all the classic candies in a circle formation around the popcorn and enjoy!

BOARD INGREDIENTS

6 cups popped, buttered popcorn

1 jumbo lollipop

1 bag Twizzlers

1 bag M&M's

1 box Good & Plenty

1 bag wax soda bottle candy

1 bag Skittles

1 bag Circus Peanuts candy

8 striped candy sticks

VALENTINE'S DAY STRAWBERRIES AND CHOCOLATE

Cheese, chocolates, and juicy strawberries are symbols of true love, at least at the Grace-Filled Homestead. This board is filled with all the favorites for your loved ones.

BOARD INGREDIENTS

1 Strawberry Brie Puff Pastry (recipe follows)

12 white chocolate–covered strawberries

2 cups puppy chow snack mix*

1 cup strawberry chocolate-covered pretzels

6 strawberry jam cookies

Crackers or crusty bread

*This is a premade coated-cereal snack also known as Muddy Buddies.

BOARD DIRECTIONS

Place Strawberry Brie Puff Pastry in the middle of your board, then surround it with the chocolate-covered fruit, puppy chow, pretzels, and cookies. Serve with your favorite crackers or crusty bread.

STRAWBERRY BRIE PUFF PASTRY

INGREDIENTS

1 frozen puff pastry sheet

16 oz. brie

1 egg

¼ cup strawberry jam

2 T. powdered sugar

DIRECTIONS

Set the frozen puff pastry out to thaw for 20 minutes. Preheat the oven to 400°F. On a floured surface, unfold the partially-thawed pastry. Using a rolling pin, roll to approximately 14 inches long, dusting with flour as needed. Using a 2- or 3-inch heart-shaped cookie cutter, cut out a heart in the middle of the pastry. Place brie in the center of the puff pastry atop the cutout and trim an inch off the corners. Fold the pastry over the cheese to cover it, tucking as needed. In a small dish, beat the egg to create an egg wash. Brush egg onto the pastry to coat. Flip the pastry-wrapped brie over so the ends are underneath and the pastry heart cutout is on top. Fill the heart with the strawberry jam. Bake 25 minutes or until golden; allow to stand 10 minutes before serving. Sprinkle with powdered sugar.

YIELD: 8 SERVINGS

VALENTINE'S PEPPERONI ROSES

A dozen roses ... yes, please! But forget the expensive cut flowers that wilt away in a week. Pepperoni roses are all the rage, and for good reason. The men especially love this valentine board. Pepperoni roses are simple to make and delicious to serve with cheese and crackers. This is love at first sight and makes the ultimate charcuterie board.

BOARD DIRECTIONS

Lay four large pepperoni pieces in a row, slightly overlapping. Fold the entire row in half from the bottom up. Roll, starting at the right side of row, until you have a flower bud shape. Secure the rose with a toothpick and add a sage leaf to each side of the rose, securing these with the same toothpick. Arrange the twelve roses in a bouquet formation on the board. Cut the onion bulbs off the green onions and place the long green parts on the board as the rose stems, just beneath the blooms. Cover the bottom of the board with cheese and crackers. Enjoy!

BOARD INGREDIENTS

48 large pepperoni slices
24 sage leaves
12 green onions
24 slices cheese
24 crackers

ACKNOWLEDGMENTS

Thank you to all of you who are reading this book and joining in on the fun of the charcuterie board. I hope you enjoyed the journey through these pages as much as I have. There have been so many amazing people who have helped this book come to life.

CJ—*How is this our life?* In high school we had dreams of our future, but we never imagined all of God's goodness, grandbabies, or even the goats. Thank you for your love, stability, and willingness for adventure. I can't wait to grow old with you.

To my kiddos, Colton, Cameron, Isaiah, Sophia, Madalyn, and Jadyn—You are my heavy lifters, literally. You show up for the work, the hugs, and whatever is needed, whether it's hay day, praying, cooking for us, moving your grandparents, or mowing their lawn, you are selfless and brilliant. I am beyond blessed to even know you, let alone be your mom.

Riley and Walker, my precious grandbabies—You are pure sunshine. Your smiles and hugs are one of God's greatest gifts. Thank you for the joy and giggles.

To my siblings, Debbie, Don, and John—It's been an unforgettable year filled with tears and joy, and I can't thank you enough for your support and prayers every step of the way.

To my mother-in-love, Cindy—Thank you for raising the most amazing man a girl could ask for. You have spoiled my kids rotten, and now you are also a wonderful great-grandma. I love your sass as much as your holiday spreads!

To my beautiful sisters-in-love—I am beyond blessed to have you not only as family but as dear friends. Kendra, Kristen, Jamie, and Nikki, I truly appreciate your constant support and love.

To my brothers-in-law, Marc and Travis—You are saints. Words cannot express how much I appreciate your support and help this past year after losing my parents.

The LYLAS girl gang: Dee, Steph, Raelyn, Sue, Tonya, and Lisa—Who knew that this rebellious group of middle schoolers would turn into prayer warriors supporting each other through life's toughest journeys. You all are the best. Thank you for everything this past year.

Jenni at Illuminate Literary—Thank you for your wisdom and guidance through every step of the publishing process. You are brilliant, and it's a joy to work with you.

Ruth, Hope, Heather, Adrienne, Heidi, and the Harvest House Publishers team—Thank you for your friendship, insight, and endless hours of work. I truly appreciate you.

To my online friends, shop owners, and homestead community—Words cannot express my appreciation of your support, kind emails, purchases of our products, and coming out to visit at events. Our relationships are the real deal and make what we do so fun. Thank you from the bottom of my heart!

ABOUT LANA

Lana is an author, podcast host, college professor, backyard farmer, and the author of *The Grace-Filled Homestead* and *The Grace-Filled Homestead Cookbook*. More than twenty years ago, Lana and her husband, CJ, decided to ditch their fast-paced hustle for the simple life. They found a small farm on the edge of town, moved their four little children into a hundred-year-old fixer-upper, and began to focus on God, goats, and gardens at the Grace-Filled Homestead.

Follow Lana's fun barnyard animal videos on Instagram and TikTok, and draw inspiration from her recipes and DIY blog at lanastenner.com. There, you'll also discover the Graham and Goat Studio Shop, the Backyard Farm Academy classes, and the *Grace-Filled Grit* podcast. Lana is grateful for God's grace and uses her time helping others strengthen their faith, family, and farm.

 CONNECT WITH LANA

www.lanastenner.com   TikTok @lanastennerandgoatgang
IG and FB @lanastenner   Pinterest @lanastennerhomestead